Their Pain but God's Promises

By Miracle Bridges

Front cover created by Jason Moore

Designed by Jazzy Kitty Publishing

Logo designs by Andre M. Saunders and Leroy Grayson

Editor Jazzy Kitty Publishing

© 2017 Miracle Bridges

ISBN: 978-0-9988433-1-5

Library of Congress Control Number: 2017937680

All rights reserved. This book is protected by the copyright laws of the United States of America. This book may not be copied or reprinted for commercial gain or profit. The use of short quotations or occasional page copying for personal or group study is permitted and encouraged. Permission will be granted upon request. Some actual scriptures were used. For Worldwide Distribution, available in Paperback and eBook. Printed in the United States of America. Published Jazzy Kitty Greetings Marketing & Publishing dba Jazzy Kitty Publishing utilizing Microsoft Publishing Software.

ACKNOWLEDGMENTS

I would first like to thank God for giving me my purpose and gift as a writer. All glory goes to Him. A sincere thank you to my husband Jason Bridges who helped endorsed my first book.

To my Sister-in-Christ Toya Poplar whose words and prayers helped me to stay focused and my New Life SDA church family.

To my Mother-in-Law Anjanette Taylor for her no sugar-coated words of motivation; my Uncle Brian Booker with Brian B. Photography; and all of my family and friends who believed in me and encouraged me to push toward my goals, and to walk into my calling as a writer and a poet. I thank God for you all and I love you with all my heart!

Special thank to Jason Moore and his wife the overseers of the profound ministry "They Overcame By" and M2PH Marketing Group.

Finally, thanks to Jazzy Kitty Publishing for all their hard work and patience.

DEDICATIONS

I would like to dedicate this book to people like me. For people that have been broken many times and in many different areas of their lives. For those of you that felt like you were too deep in sin, too filthy for God to pull you out and use you for His glory. Also, for those family members who became victims of generational curses.

I dedicate this book to those of you who put on a mask of perfection, but behind the scenes are struggling and refuses to give anyone a glimpse into your life because of what other people may think. I want you to know that God can take anyone that desires Him and clean them up. He can build you up to become the child of God that He created you to be. You can be broken in a million pieces, but God has the power and the ability to make you whole again. So, as you read this book, just remember that I dedicate this book to you and I believe indeed that you are more than a conqueror!

TABLE OF CONTENTS

INTRODUCTION... i
CHAPTER 1 -   The Beginning of the Family Tree 01
CHAPTER 2 -   Life & Death 17
CHAPTER 3 -   God Works in a Mysterious Way 32
CHAPTER 4 -   Times Changes, Lives Changes 37
CHAPTER 5 -   Time Flies by Fast 46
CHAPTER 6 -   Pressure and Pain 54
CHAPTER 7 -   Time of Trouble 63
CHAPTER 8 -   Separated and Different - Part 1 Tyra............66
  -   Part 2 Myra 71
  -   Part 3 Lacie 77
CHAPTER 9 -   Nothing Happens by Accident 81
CHAPTER 10 - What's Done in the Dark Comes to the Light...............91
CHAPTER 11 - Things Get Worse Before They Get Better 97
ABOUT THE AUTHOR..108

INTRODUCTION

So, as I sit here and think about how to write the perfect introduction for this book. I realize that there is no perfect way to write an introduction other than to just be real and introduce it. Some people probably won't be able to handle the details of the characters in this book, but believe it or not, these are real-life problems that people face. At least one of the characters in this book will relate to someone.

Some people are really battling with brokenness, drug abuse, having children out of wedlock, the death of a loved one, generational curses, and so forth. Too many times people become afraid of revealing their mess. They get saved and act as if they're perfect and never went through anything or have ever done anything wrong. When in reality, the very thing that they were delivered from is the very thing that someone they know could be battling with. You see, sometimes it's so easy to forget where God has brought us from. It's easy to keep our skeletons in a closet when our testimony has the power to draw others to Jesus. It's easy to look at someone and judge them when you really have no idea what that person has or is going through in their life. It's easy to want to give up when things get hard in your marriage or in your relationships with other people, but I encourage everyone who picks up this book to love people genuinely and to share your testimony with others because you never know how God can use your mess as a message and turn you into the messenger that He designed you to be. Revelation 12:11 says, "They overcame by the power of their testimony." Realize that you have power!

CHAPTER 1

The Beginning of the Family Tree

Mable Jenkins was an awesome lady that didn't take any crap. She was a mother that carried most of the weight in a bad marriage. She was married to Mr. James Jenkins who was a wannabe player that really messed around on Mable. People wondered why she had stuck around for so long, but she believed that marriage was not only a commitment to James but that it was a commitment to God.

James worked at an auto shop with Mr. Pete for about 15 years. James and Pete graduated from a junior college together with a degree in Auto Mechanics. They figured they would open a shop together. Mable didn't really care where he worked as long as he was bringing the money in to take care of the bills. Now, of course, she didn't always think that way. Mable was 19 when she married James. She had already made up her mind that she was in love and that she was going to do everything in her power to be with him. She would sneak out at night just to go to the Friday night football games with him. Her brothers tried to cover for her but lying to their parents was like committing suicide. Papa Joe had no problems with beating them until they turned blue. Now that she was 19 she felt like she could make her own decisions. However, her parents didn't approve of their marriage. So they got married at the downtown courthouse. Mable still happy and felt like a grown woman. She felt as if she had just signed a contract to experience a whole different world and way of living.

Mable parents met after a huge tornado hit Nashville Tennessee. Her mother had lost everything. Feeling hopeless and afraid she went down to the American Helpers United Organization to get some assistance. They turned her away twice, saying that her house was too old and that if the tornado didn't destroy it, it would soon be destroyed just by a strong gust of wind. Being sarcastic of course, but still turning her away. It hurt her at first, but she had to remind herself that God is all-knowing and that her house is built on the rock meaning Jesus Christ and that He is her shelter in the time of the storm even though the tornado was indeed a terrible storm. She knew her house needed working on badly and didn't need anyone to remind her of that. That house was passed down from generation to generation and now she had lost it to that horrible tornado. Walking away saying a silent prayer to herself she was caught off guard by a young gentleman calling her name.

Mrs. Willis, "Yes! she replied."

"Excuse me Ma'am, but I overheard you talking to my supervisor about your house being ruined and you needed some assistance."

"Yes, I do, but they turned me away."

"Yes Ma'am, I saw that and me personally, I don't think it's right."

"Yeah, it's not right Sir, but I know God will make a way. I remember reading this Bible scripture that says He will never leave me nor forsake me or put more on me that I can bear. So, I'll just…"

Interrupting her he said, "I know you just met me, but I do have an extra bedroom you can use until you get yourself back on track."

"Sir! Listen, my name is Joseph, but just call me Joe."

"Well, Joe I appreciate it, but I don't wanna be a burden to you or your wife."

"Wife! No, Ma'am, I'm not married."

"Well, your kids."

"Oh no, Ma'am no kids, but I would love to have some one day."

"Look, Joe that's really kind of you, but I have nothing. No money, no food, and as you can see I only got the clothes on my back."

"Did I ask you for anything?"

"You said you know that Jesus will provide for you. So, how do you know He didn't send me to be a blessing to you?"

She started to reply, "Well..." but he cut her off again, "trust me, Mrs. Willis."

"Stop calling me Mrs. I am not married either. Now listen, I will stay with you, but no funny business."

"Ma'am I'm here to help you, not hinder you. I get off in a few minutes, but meanwhile how about you follow me; I will show you where you can get some clothes. They're not new clothes, but people have donated them to those in need right now."

"Thank you so much, Joe."

An hour later they arrived at his home. He lived in a nice neighborhood near the projects, but it was still nice.

"Wow, you have a nice house."

Considering the shack she lived in anything would have been a nice place to her, but she had always been grateful for what she had.

She always held on to that scripture that said don't put away riches on earth. Put them up in Heaven.

You see, she was brought up in the church and everything in her holds on to the promises of God. Joe was also brought up in the church, but left the church after being criticized about his peers and other wrong decisions he made. Instead of telling him the right way, they tore him down with their fouls words and used scriptures to do it. I guess they didn't read the part in the Bible that said, judge no one unless you be judged.

"Well, here goes your room Mrs. Willis. There is a bathroom and a walk-in closet if you need anything just let me know."

"Well in that case, I need you to stop calling me Mrs. Willis; I am not married and besides most people call me Mae."

"Ok, will do Mae. Are you hungry?"

"I sure am! I'm so hungry that I'm full." They both laughed hysterically.

"Well, in that case, I guess you can't fit anything else in there." They proceeded to the kitchen.

As soon as she walked in, she noticed the homemade wooden table in the center of the kitchen that reminded her of the table that her grandad had made when she was younger.

"Thank you so much. You seem like a nice person."

"Well thank you so much, Mae you're not so bad yourself," he said as she smiled at him.

She noticed for the first time how handsome he was. He was about 6'1, 190 pounds, with brown curly hair, a pretty white smile, and a deep but pleasant voice.

Finding herself now staring at him she managed to blurt out, "Why are you not married?"

"Well, I just haven't found the right one. It seems like every woman I meet standards are either too high or their lifestyle is totally against my type."

"What is your type, if I may ask? Not that I'm interested or anything I'm just wondering why a handsome man like yourself is single."

"So, you think I'm handsome?"

"Oh gosh, just answer the question."

They both laughed while he replied, "My type is a nice strong-minded,

Christian lady that will back her man up 100%, that don't care about how much I own, and who would love to get married one day and have a family."

"Well, that's what every woman wants."

"Not the women that I have been meeting. (LOL) I guess when God is ready He will send the right one for me until then I'll keep my eyes open."

Giving her this weird look, he replied, "Good night Beautiful. I meant Mae." As he turned away to leave the kitchen she smiled, feeling warm inside.

Before he got too far out of her sight she called out to him, "Would you like to pray together before you go to bed. I mean if you don't want to I won't be offended."

Before she could say anything else he grabbed both of her hands and asked, "Me first or you first?"

"Me," she replied.

She bowed her head and started to pray out loud, *"Dear Heavenly Father thank You for providing for me. Thank You for blessing Joe so he could be a blessing to me. I know that Your promises are true and know that You are the One and True God that sent His Only Son, Jesus Christ to die for us. So, thank You, Lord. Please bless Joe in every aspect of his life and may Your Will be done. In Jesus' Name Amen."*

As he started to pray, he tightened the grip on her hands, *"Dear Lord, I come to You realizing that You hold All Power in Your hands. I thank You for protecting Mae and delivering her from that storm Lord. I ask that You forgive us for our sins and shortcomings and bless us where You see fit. Help me to be a good person and an even better friend to Mae during her time of need. These things I ask in Jesus' Name Amen."* Little did they know God was already answering their prayers. They smiled at each other and departed ways.

The next few weeks went by and Joe noticed that every morning Mae would get up, read her Bible, and sing softly around the house.

He asked curiously, "Is this something you do every morning?"

"Yes, it is," she replied, "I use to do this every morning. I would get up and have my morning devotion while I sat on the porch swing and talked to God. It felt like He was sitting right next to me. Even when it rained I would sit on the front porch and never mind..." her voice trailed off.

"No, what were you going to say?"

"Well, when I was a little girl, my dad used to tell me that when I did bad things I made the angels cry. So, I would sit there and repent of everything that I've ever done wrong and I would even pray for other people to repent and live right as well. Whether it was true or not about making the angels cry, I did notice things changing."

"Like what?" he replied.

"Like my neighbor, Charlie; he was a heavy drinker that use to beat his wife. He never wanted her talking to me. He said that I was such a Jesus-addict and he didn't want her around me. I just laughed it off. Of course, she used to sneak away and talk to me anyway especially after he would beat her up then go to the bar. One time, she was pregnant and he didn't know it. He beat her so bad that she had a miscarriage on my bathroom floor. Blooded up my favorite bathroom rug set and my best towels, but those things were materialistic so I didn't care. All I cared about was her safety and his soul. After cleaning her up, we prayed together, and I held her while she cried. After that, I walked her home before he had gotten back. Day after day, we would get together and pray until one day she finally got the courage to leave him. She moved to Maryland and got saved. She worked at a center that helped homeless children find families and helped them learn different trades. Charlie continued to drink and drink while I continued to pray and pray. A day before Christmas he had a bad car accident down the street from the house. I knew it was bad when I saw them struggling to get him from out of the car. I was told that the car flipped nine times and it was only by the grace of God that he survived. I knew then that God had heard my prayers. One day, the Holy Spirit impressed on my heart to go to the hospital and see him, so I did. When I walked into his room he was asleep, so I just stood next to his bed and prayed for him."

As I was finishing up my prayer, I felt his hand grab mine and he softly said, "Thank you for coming. Can you tell me more about the God you were just praying to?" I shockingly said yes and took a seat in the chair that was near the foot of his bed. That night I stayed there for almost four hours. We prayed, we laughed, and we even cried. After visiting him for about two weeks he told me that he wanted to give his life to Jesus Christ. My mind was blown and I was reminded that there is no sin too big enough to make God stop loving you.

A week later he was released from the hospital. I took him home and had a home cooked meal prepared for him. Little did he know, Sarah had flown into town to see him when I called and told her the good news about him giving his life to Jesus. I guess she wanted to see for herself or maybe she knew he would change one day. That probably explains why she never filed for divorce, but instead just separated herself from the problems. She knew we fight not against flesh and blood, but against principalities.

Miracle Bridges

Sarah had only been gone for six months. When he walked into the house the first thing he saw was Sarah standing there with a belly just as big as she was. Little did he know Sarah was 10 weeks pregnant when she left him and moved to Maryland. She didn't want to lose the baby that she was carrying due to his drunken rants and raves, so she figured leaving him was the only way to save their child and possibly herself. She walked over, or should I say waddled over to him and hugged him so tight that he would have needed CPR by the time she was done.

As tears dripped down his face he just kept saying to her, "Please forgive me and please forgive me for everything that I have ever done to you."

She looked into his eyes and said, "I forgive you. I forgive you because Christ has forgiven me."

"Sarah, I love you so much; let's start over. Me, you, and the baby…"

She smiled, interrupted his plea and said, "Actually babies meaning more than one. We are having twins." The look in his eyes was one that I had never seen before. He was indeed happy to become a father.

Sarah ended up moving back with Charlie and every week they attended church with me. They participated in Bible studies and Charlie mentored some of the children at the local detention home.

One day he came home from the detention center. He walked into the house and followed the little tracks that looked like water. They led him into the bathroom where he found Sarah laying on the floor in pain. Her water had broken. He quickly called me on the phone sounding frantic. I told him to calm down and I would be right there. I called the ambulance and they rushed her to St. Andrews Hospital.

She arrived there not a minute sooner. One of the babies came out barely making it to the Delivery Room. The second baby came out two minutes later.

"Wow! Two baby boys! which they named Andrew and Andre." Andrew came out first weighing 5 pounds 8 ounces and Andre weighed 5 pounds 6 ounces. I was so truly happy for them.

Three days later, Sarah was released from the hospital. They stayed for about three months then moved back to Maryland. Until this day, we still keep in touch. So, you see, praying for people really works.

God said, "Whatever you believe in My Son Name' you will receive."

Joe who had been staring at Mae the entire time finally said, "You are just an awesome lady. I love your Spirit and your faith in God. If I didn't know any better, I would even say I think I love you."

Mae's eyes widened, "Love me? Are you serious Joe?"

"Yes, I'm serious Mae. I mean I just never met anyone like you. You are so mind blowing in so many ways." Looking at his wristwatch he noticed that it was time for him to go to work.

"Well, I will see you later, I have to head out to work. You behave yourself, Little Woman," he said and gave her a smile and headed for the door.

After he left, she found herself thinking hard about what he had just said. She was so excited because she hadn't heard the words I love you in a long time. To be honest she felt the same way that he did although she didn't tell him. It was something about him that she really liked which made her feel safe in his presence. In fact, she was so excited that she decided to cook dinner that night. She cooked cabbage, fried chicken, mac-n-cheese, cornbread from scratch, rice, and a homemade pound cake.

When he got home from work and walked into the house he noticed the smell immediately. He walked into the kitchen quickly and found Mae in a used apron that she had gotten from the donated clothes. She had her hair pulled back and dressed up nicely. She smiled and welcomed him like he was at a restaurant.

"Welcome to Mae's Diner; dinner is served," she laughed as he smiled and said thank you.

That night they talked about his family background and her family background. Before you knew it, it was three hours later. Honestly, they didn't want to depart from each other's presence.

"Well, that was delicious Mae. I had no idea that you were such a good cook. I could definitely get use to that. I wish I met you a long time ago." They both laughed.

Mae stopped laughing and became very serious. "Joe, earlier when you said you love me. Did you really mean it? Or better yet, how did you mean it?"

"I thought you would have known by now Mae."

"Know what Joe?"

"That I love you. Like I really love you. I know when we first met that you weren't interested in being in a relationship, but I fell in love with you from the first time I saw you. You know, I actually prayed about you, well about us. That if you were the right woman for me then send me a sign."

"Well, maybe this is a sign."

Looking into his eyes she stood up and grabbed his hand and said, "The feeling is mutual."

"Mae, are you saying…"

Interrupting him she said, "Yes Joe, I feel the same way about you. It's funny because last night I had this dream that we got married. That your boss was there and it was such a beautiful wedding."

Putting his finger on her lips to shut her up he replied, "Why not just make it a reality."

He reached into his pocket and pulled out a ring. Little did she know he had bought a ring two weeks ago and was waiting for the right time to ask her for her hand in marriage. So, I guess this was the right time because he got on one knee and softly asked her to marry him. She said yes and cried tears of joy. She hugged him and couldn't believe that it was really happening. What was even more amazing was that Joe had told his boss his plans to propose to Mae. Without him knowing that his boss wife was a wedding planner, she wanted to be a blessing to them by doing their wedding for free. They didn't have to spend a dime. It was beautiful. They had red and white roses everywhere like it was a scene from out of a movie. They had 75 guests; it was a beautiful wedding. Mae felt like she was on cloud 9.

The week before the wedding Joe had gotten a promotion to General Manager and had gotten extra vacation time. They went to the Bahamas on their honeymoon. When they arrived there, they were treated like royalty. They had sparkling grape juice and apple cider on ice waiting for them with an all you can eat buffet.

About two hours later, they went back to the room to relax. That night they made passionate love to each other for the first time. They seemed inseparable. Mae loved that man with all her heart and he loved her as well and nothing could ever come between them.

When they arrived back in Tennessee after the honeymoon they were exhausted. Since he had two more days off all they did was sleep.

About 8 weeks later Mae was doing her morning routine. Singing and doing her devotional until suddenly she got sick. The look she had on her face was a look of disgust. Like she had just ridden a roller coaster on a full stomach. She immediately ran to the toilet, throwing up everything that she had eaten for breakfast. Noticing that something was wrong she went to her room to change her clothes. She walked to the nearest corner store which was only half a mile away and purchased a pregnancy test. Not really knowing what to do, she went home and waited for Joe to wake up.

When he walked into the kitchen he noticed she was sitting down drinking a cup of decaf coffee. Now knowing his wife, the only time she drank coffee was when she was nervous about something.

"Mae, what's wrong?"

"Why would you assume that something is wrong Sweetie?"

"Because you're my wife and I know the only time you drink coffee is when you are nervous about something, so what's going on?"

"Ok Joe, you got me. Well, I may be pregnant, but please don't be mad."

"Mad!!! Baby, I would never be mad at something like that! Besides, you know that I've always wanted kids. So, did you take a test or go to the doctor?"

"No, but I bought a test this morning. I'm just afraid to take it. Will you come in the bathroom with me while I take it?"

"Of course, Babe."

They both walked to the master bathroom. Mae sat on the toilet and took a sample of her urine in a little cup. Then she carefully read and followed the instructions on the box. She waited and just as clear as day it read positive. She looked at him with a nervous look on her face.

He looked at her and replied, "So what does it say Mae, don't keep me waiting."

"It says that I am pregnant Joe."

Joe excitedly got down on his knees. He hugged and kissed his wife and told her that everything was going to be okay. She smiled at him. They finally left the bathroom crying tears of joy and praying.

Every day that Joe came home from work he would give Mae foot massages and stomach rubs. She cooked for him and made sure the house was clean. She hardly ever had morning sickness so her pregnancy went well.

Nine months came in went in what seemed like a blink of an eye. Her due date was December 24th but she had the baby on Christmas Day. Wow, what a gift for them. A baby boy named Joseph Jr. He was 6 pounds 3 ounces. She only had to stay in the hospital for two days. He was a good baby and was very healthy. He slept through the night and only cried if he was either wet or hungry. Joe and Mae seemed like the happiest couple alive. Joe was indeed a good father.

Joseph wasn't quite 9-months-old before Mae had gotten pregnant with their second child. This time her pregnancy seemed long. Her feet stayed swollen and she had the craziest food cravings ever. One time, she ate pickles and cereal as a midnight snack.

Two weeks later, she was in the grocery store and while standing at the register paying for her groceries she felt a gush. When she looked down she saw a small puddle and instantly knew what was happening. The cashier called the ambulance quickly. Mae grabbed her cell phone and called Joe.

Breathing heavily, she managed to say, "Joe meet me at the hospital my water just broke and it's time." Without hesitation, Joe hung up the phone and rushed to the hospital.

As soon as he got there, they were just bringing her in. They took her straight to the delivery room and within two hours, a baby boy came out crying loudly. He had a head full of hair and weighed 6 pounds 9 ounces. He was a big baby. Mae and Joe named him Jonathan. Johnathan was a good baby as well. He cried a bit more than Joseph Jr. did, but he was still a good baby. Mae was exhausted the first two weeks that she had been back home from the hospital, so Joe had taken off work to help her care for the boys, but after 4 weeks, he had to go back to work.

Now having two children, time went by fast. They had a big celebration for Johnathan's 2nd birthday. Joe parents came in from Texas to spend a week with them and to give them a break from the boys. They truly did appreciate it and enjoyed every minute of it.

When the day came for them to leave, Joe's mother gave him a kiss on the cheek and jokingly asked him when they were going to give her a granddaughter. They both laughed as he tooked her bags to the car. His dad came out talking loudly about how much fun he had and how he hated to go home. Joe had a very close relationship with his parents.

They said their goodbyes and went back into the house to tend to the boys. Mae got Joseph and Joe got Johnathan. They gave them a bath and put them to bed. Before you knew it, the boys were old enough to start school. Joseph was 6 and Johnathan was 5. They were so excited to start school. Every morning the kids would get up with Mae and pray before heading to the bus. Joe always made it a habit to tell the kids he was proud of them for their good behavior and good grades in school. And he told them that they were kings in the making. It was one of the cutest and most encouraging moments I had ever seen.

One day, something very hilarious happened. Johnathan's teacher was seven months pregnant with a girl. Johnathan came home and ran to his mom and dad then put his hands-on Mae's stomach.

He looked up at her and said, "Mommy, Mrs. Berlow has a girl in her stomach, can you go get a girl in your stomach to?" Mae looked at Joe in shock from Johnathan's question.

Joe burst out laughing and said, "Well, I guess it's time for us to go shopping for a girl." Mae smiled at her husband and at her two little boys.

Within three months, Mae found out that she was indeed pregnant. It was not surprising to find out that it was a girl. Everyone kept speaking it into existence. You see, life and death is in the power of the tongue and sometimes you can repeat something over and over or pray for something so much that it will actually happens. Mae spent most of the time sleeping during her third pregnancy. The boys spent a lot of time at the After School Program. They were having a ball though. They played basketball, soccer, and even learned how to play the piano. Knowing that they had a sister on the way they just couldn't keep quiet. They told everyone they knew that mommy bought a baby girl for her stomach. It was so funny to think that they thought she bought a girl for her stomach. Sometimes right before bed the boys would come in and rub Mae's stomach and pray for their little sister. For some reason, those boys loved to pray. I guess whatever you do in front of your kids they will soon pick up on. Whether it is smoking, drinking, cursing, fighting, acting wild, or whatever it may be. However, in this case, it was praying. You see, children idolized their parents which mean you should be very cautious about what you do around them.

You should raise a child in the way that they should go.

Don't tell your children not to curse, drink, or have premarital sex when you are doing it right in front of them. We should lead by example.

CHAPTER 2
Life & Death

Joe and Mae did have some good boys indeed. When it was time for her to go into labor with their little sister the boys were really confused about what was going on. They were sitting at the table having dinner when suddenly Mae's water broke. Having had went through this twice already she knew what was going on, but at the same time, it was surprising because her due date was July 7th and it was June 30th. Joe helped her get dressed and put her in the car. Their neighbor watched the kids for them while they headed to the hospital. Joseph Jr. kept asking if mommy was going to the store to get the baby out her stomach, he was totally confused about where a baby came from. Not that he cared anyway, he was just happy to be getting a little sister.

Mae arrives at the hospital at 7:38 pm and had Mable at 10:24 pm that night. Two days later, she was released from the hospital and the boys were there waiting at the door for her and baby Mable to arrive. The boys were so excited. They both just wanted to hold her and kiss all over her. It's something about a newborn baby that attracts everyone. The boys were great with Mable. They would take turns feeding her and helped Mae with the diapers. Baby Mable was a good baby, but she was spoiled indeed. Everyone loved her and always wanted to hold her. When she cried, they held her; when she laughed, they held her. She was like a human magnet. While Joe would be at work and the boys at school, Mae would sing hymnals to Mable and put her to sleep. Mable seemed so sweet. She was a quiet child. Well, for now, that was.

When Mable was 7, Mae and Joe put her in Girl Scouts. One day Mable ate all her Girl Scout Cookies. She honestly thought that they were for her. She had to do extra chores to pay the money back to her parents for covering her cookie payment, but it was definitely a lesson learned.

Then when she was 10, she snuck into Jonathan's room and broke his guitar string after he told her several times not to touch his guitar. Mable was very rebellious growing up and nobody understood why. She would just do mean things for the fun of it. She had stolen money several times from her parents, lied to get her way, lie to get out of trouble, and started fights in school. Mae and Joe did the best they could with Mable. They thought it was maybe because she was the youngest and being the only girl, she got everything she wanted. As much as Mae and Joe read the Bible they must have missed the part where it says, spare the rod spoil the child. That's why when Mable decided at the age of 19 that she was going to get married, they didn't argue with her and try to stop her, they just simply didn't approve. It was something about James that Joe didn't like or maybe it was the fact that he just didn't want to let his baby girl go. Mable was the first one to move out of her parent's house.

One year later, Johnathan moved and got married as well to a woman from New York named Janice Taylor. She was a very interesting lady who came from a wealthy lady. They met while Johnathan was on a mission trip in New York.

Joseph Jr. stayed with Mae and Joe until he was in his late 30's. He had plans to move out but it was mostly all talk. A plan without action is just words. Joseph Jr. would hang out all times of night and wouldn't come back for days. One night, he got into an argument with Joe about not being a man and not keeping a job. He left the house mad and decided to go to this bar called Lucky's to have a few drinks, but little did he know the night wouldn't end so lucky. While he was on his way home, he was going 67 mph in a 30 mph speed zone. Approaching a curve, he swerved into the opposite lane not realizing it and crash into an oncoming car, killing himself along with two adults and an 8-year-old girl. That was soon to be discovered as Joe's old boss, his wife, and their granddaughter. They had come from her ballet recital. The impact killed them instantly.

When Joe and Mae found out they were devastated. Joe had been retired for about 8 years and always kept in touch with his old boss. The last time he saw them was about a month before the accident. Mae had invited them over for dinner. Not only did they lose their oldest son, but they lost two close friends. When Mable heard it on the news she couldn't believe it and was devastated as well.

Earlier that day, Mable had found out that she and James were having their first child and couldn't wait to gather the family together to tell them. Now her day became dark and depressing. She had just spoken to him a few days ago and he told her that he was going to give up all the drinking after the New Years', so he could stay focus and keep a job. Little did he know he wasn't gonna make it to see New Years.

You see, tomorrow isn't guaranteed to anyone. Actually, the next minute isn't guaranteed to anyone. That why it's important for us to look at the way are living, the way we think and even the way we act. Saying we are Christians, doesn't just mean going to church every week. It's everything, your entire lifestyle. That's why the Bible says choose ye this day whom ye will serve. You may not have until tomorrow to stop the fornication, doing drugs, gossiping, fighting, sleeping with married people, cursing, stealing, and killing etc. So, that's why it's important to repent daily.

After the funeral, Joe spent weeks just lying in bed. He didn't want to eat or sleep. He just laid there miserable and feeling like everything was his fault. Mae tried her best to brighten his spirits, but it was pointless.

Not even four months after the accident, Joe to had died. The autopsy said he died from natural causes, but if it was up to Mae to determine how he died she would have said it was from a broken heart. A lot of people fail to realize that depression can kill a person. It's never healthy to worry, especially about things that you have no control over. That's why it's important to stay rooted in the Word of God. You can receive joy and peace in Him.

Mae was grieving badly. Therefore, Mable and Johnathan came home to take over the funeral arrangements. It was just too much for Mae to go through. Within one year, her husband, son, and two close friends have passed away. She had to constantly remind herself that God knows what's best and that this too shall pass. Mable and James decided to just move back home with Mae and take care of her. That way he could still work at the shop which was even closer now since they moved in with Mae. At first, Mae didn't want James living in her house because she always felt some kind of way about him ever since Mable decided to marry him at the age of 19. Now having him in the house, she soon got over it. Besides Mable was now almost 7 months pregnant with a baby girl which would be Mae's first grandchild. Mable wished that her father would have had a chance to meet his first grandchild, but everything happens for a reason.

When Mable went into labor, James was two hours late getting there; 10 minutes later and he would have missed the birth of his first child. The baby came out crying as loud as she could. She was a beautiful baby, weighing 5 pounds 9 ounces. Mable named her Lacie Jenkins. Mae was the first one to hold Lacie. She would never forget the day that Lacie was born. It was July 27th and her first grandchild was finally here. As she held Lacie, tears dripped down her cheek. She couldn't believe that her baby girl had just had her own baby girl and even better, she was there to witness it all.

After they were released from the hospital, James spent most of his time working. It seemed like Mable was doing all the work alone, well with the help of Mae of course. Mable was so excited to be a mother and Mae was excited to be a grandmother.

Although James worked a lot, things were still going well until a few months went by. Things started to seem a little weird. James wasn't spending hardly any time at home. Mable asked James plenty of times why he wasn't spending more time at home and his reply always referred to work. She just brushed it off counting that they needed the money. Mae tried to talk to Mable about being a little bit more firmer with him, so he could spend more time at home, so she started to nag him about it. It must have worked because he started to spend a bit more time at home. Although he was home like she asked him all he ever seemed to do was eat and watch TV. He hardly ever spent any time with Lacie. He felt like it was the mother's job to tend to the baby and the father's job to work and bring home the income. Mae didn't like that at all, but what could she really say. Her daughter was now married to this man who was a workaholic and had no morals at all. He never really attended church unless it was for a funeral or a wedding, but that didn't stop Mae from praying for him though. After all, Mable was her daughter and James was still her son-n-law.

About five months later, the same thing started back up again. He would work from sunrise to sunset. After a while, Mable just gave up. She

Miracle Bridges

knew what type of man James was before she even married him and that's what I don't understand. Some people get into relationships with people knowing that they're not right for them and saying in the back of their mind that maybe I can change them. Maybe, I can mold them into who I want them to become. First of all, you can't change people that don't want to be changed. Secondly, human power is not enough to make a person change; only God can truly change a person. Think about it though, He is the one that created us. Mable knew a lot about James, but after a while, people change and she would soon to find out.

One morning Mable wasn't feeling well. She had been feeling really weak and tired for the past two weeks. So, she decided to go see a doctor. When she arrived at the doctor she got checked in, but it wasn't long before the doctor called her into his office. She told him how she had been feeling. He ran a few tests on her and to her surprise and his surprise she was pregnant again. She had just had Lacie not even two years ago and now she was pregnant again. Not that she was sad or anything, but just shocked. After she left the doctor's office she went back to the house and told Mae the news.

Mae replied, "I could have told you that you were pregnant Mable."

"How did you know Mama?"

"Easy, people just don't eat pickles and cereal on a regular basis." They looked at each other and both laughed.

Mable said excitedly, "I hope it's a boy that way I can have my boy and girl and be done with having kids."

Mae just smiled and said, "Whatever it is, I'm sure you will love it the same."

Not even two minutes later, James came home on his lunch break. She wanted to tell James the news about the new baby, but she kept thinking about the first time she told him she was pregnant.

He just sat there with a dumb look on his face and replied, "Am I supposed to be happy about this Mable?"

"Well excuse me, James," Mable replied, "I didn't make this baby on my own. You are my husband and we made vows to stay together for better or for worst so, deal with it. Because an abortion is not even an option."

Although Mable wasn't heavy in her Bible like Mae was, that's one thing Mable did remember that Mae taught them was taking a life of another human being was murder and she was truly against that. It was more than just one of the 10 Commandments to her. She took that very seriously.

James wiped his hand raising up to a standing position and looked Mable in her eyes and said, "You know what? It doesn't matter, I am not the one who has to be here all day to raise it." Flashing a sarcastic smile, he walked out the door.

As Mae walked into the kitchen Mable just looked at her and broke down crying. She couldn't understand how the man she had come to love and honored turned into this cold-hearted and selfish man. Mae just held her and prayed over her like she used to do Sarah after Charlie would beat her half to death. She was truly hurt by his words. She just cried and kept saying over and over that Mae and Papa Joe's judgment about James were right and that she should have listened to them. Mae knew they had had problems before, but now she saw some of their problems first hand and not just a hearsay. It was too late for her to cry and apologize now. Remembering the scene when she first told him that she was pregnant all over again made her decide not to tell him at that very moment. They had been married for years now and James attitude wasn't just going to change overnight. Mae and Mable started to pray daily for James. They would even sometimes lay hand on Mable's stomach and pray. They did the same thing every day for about four months.

Time had gone by kind of quickly for Mable and James had soon figured out that she was pregnant. Mable had formed a strong bond with her mother that she never had before. Mae even offered to go with Mable to get her sonogram, so that they could see what the gender of the baby was together.

On the way there, they passed by James job, but to their surprise, the shop was closed. Which was strange because James had gotten up early like it was a regular work day and stated boldly that he was going to work. In Mable's heart, she knew that James had been messing around on her. One of her childhood friends would call her and tell her all types of stories about James but being his wife she felt like she had something the other ladies didn't have which was his children and a marriage certificate. So, she would always cut the conversation short claiming that she had to tend to Lacie.

As they pulled up to the doctor's office Mae grabbed Mable's hand and said, "You are my daughter and I can feel what you're going through right now. Even if James is not around to be a father just know that your children will still have a Father and will always be Children of God. Don't give up Mable. Just stay in the Word and keep praying."

Mable hugged her mother and kissed her softly on the cheek. Mable knew that she had gotten to the point where she acted like she didn't care at all or let it bother her, but on the inside James always being gone really did bother her.

When they got out of the car, Mae put Lacie in her stroller and proceeded inside of the doctor's office. Mable was running a few minutes late, but they welcomed her with open arms. Mable was excited, but the doctor was even more excited. Mable had gotten much bigger since the last time he saw her and didn't understand why until he started the sonogram. Mable laid their completely shocked at the fact that she was pregnant with twin girls. She could most definitely count a baby boy out of her plans. Mae didn't really care what she had, she just loved the fact that she was going to have more grandchildren. Plus, it made her think about Sherri and Charlie's twin boys which brought back pleasant memories.

When they left the doctor's office, Mable was still in complete shock about having twin girls on the way. She knew that James always wanted a son and didn't know how he would handle the news of not having just 1 girl on the way but 2. Maybe that was why he was always so distant when it came to Lacie. You would have thought that his baby girl would have melted his heart, but the saying mama's boy and daddy's girl isn't true in every case.

As Mae and Mable left the doctor's office with baby Lacie, all Mable could think about was how disappointed James was going to be. She noticed that James had been changing a lot, but knowing the fact that she was pregnant with twins was enough to focus on. She called his cell phone, but he didn't answer, so she decided to call the shop.

"P & J Auto Shop, how may I help you?"

"Hey Pete, this is Mable. I was wondering did James get in yet? I rode passed the shop earlier but didn't see his car there."

"The shop is actually closed today, but I came in today to finish up some paperwork. James has been off work for the past two days."

"You sure he didn't come in today at all to put in a few hours of work Pete?"

"Mable, I am certain that James hasn't been by here today; I've been here all day." Feeling like an idiot, she thanked him and hung up the phone.

She quickly hung up with Pete because she didn't want to go into a deep conversation about their personal business. The fact is, he always had a tendency to pry into people's business.

You see, being in people's business with the wrong motives of wanting to know was already wrong, but he discussed everybody's business with everybody else. The Bible says that we should try to live a quiet life. Therefore, you should lift people up with your words and not tear them down. Gossiping was the very opposite of that.

Pulling up in the driveway of their home, the first thing Mable saw was James car. He had gotten back before they did from the doctor's office. One thing about James is that he knew Mable's daily schedule all too well and thought he could do what he wanted when he wanted to. But, she still had no proof on what he was doing. When she walked into the house Mable flashed a sarcastic smile and asked him how was work.

"Oh, work was really good. I had to fix a transmission and an alternator. I personally, think the lady just need a new car," he replied as he tossed a little laugh in there.

Mable looked at her mother Mae who was holding Lacie in her arms. Mae turned to leave out the room because she knew what was coming next.

Their Pain but God's Promises

"James," Mable sternly said.

"Yeah what's up?"

"I asked you how work was."

"And I told you how work was Mable. What's wrong with you?"

"What's wrong with me is that you said work was great, but the truth is you have been off for the past two days. I don't know what you have been spending your time doing or who you have been spending time with. But, all I do know is that I'm not going to continue to be your fool. Lacie is about to turn 2-years-old and you are never home. I wouldn't be surprised if you forgot the birthday of your own daughter."

"Mable, I didn't forget Lacie's birthday! Her birthday is on July 8th or is it the 9th."

"My point exactly James. You don't even know when your own daughter birthday is. All I do is sit in this house. I cook and clean while Mama and I take care of Lacie all day. Do you ever think we need some time to relax? No! Do you ever think like, hey maybe, I can keep my daughter for once while Mable takes her mother to the doctor? No! Not once have you spent quality time with your child. She and her sisters are going to grow up not knowing who you are..." Mable paused noticing what she had just said.

"Hold on hold on. What do you mean sisters Mable? I didn't want any more kids as it is and now you're saying sisters as in a plural sense. We barely can take care of Lacie, let alone more kids."

Mable having heard enough she burst out and said, "James we would have more money if you stop taking days off work to do who knows what, and as far as our children are concerned, you applied for the father position when you married me. So, it's no need to waste your breath. I didn't make Lacie or these twin girls that I'm carrying on my own. So, you need to just man up and handle your responsibilities whether you like it or not."

"So, just like that, I am supposed to be okay with everything?"

"For once James stop acting like you're the victim."

"You are just one confused woman Mable. One minute you say you want me home to spend time with the family, but then you want me to work to provide for the family as well! Which one is it Mable?"

"James there are many men who work and spend time…" Knowing that she was about to cross the line she continued to say, "unless you're providing for this family, but spend your time with another family."

"Now Mable, you are taking this way too far. I am done with this conversation. I need to focus on how I'm going to provide for you and your three kids now." Knowing that he also hurt her feelings he walked out the door slamming it behind him.

After he left, Mable just sat at the table frustrated. Mae came in and pulled out a chair to sit next to Mable.

She grabbed Mable's hand and said, "Mable you can't make a man be a man and you can't make a father be a father. You must keep your eyes on Jesus Baby. You got to remind yourself that He will never leave you nor forsake you. Although James makes you feel like you are alone, just know that you are not alone. God sees everything that's going on and people will reap what they sow. If he is out there fooling around with somebody, what makes him think that the woman he is sleeping with won't do the same thing to him?"

"Mama I understand what you're saying, but you have to realize that I am a good woman. I know you and Daddy didn't want me to get married, but that was when I was 19. I have been a faithful wife to James. A good mother and he still doesn't appreciate what I do for him."

"Mable, you are doing the best you can do. You must remember that you can't make a person change. They must want to change Mable and allow God to change them inside and out. So, just hold on to the promises of God and don't give up."

That night Mable just laid on the couch, but she eventually fell asleep. She woke up about three in the morning to a loud noise that came from the kitchen. She ran into the kitchen only to find her mother passed out on the floor unresponsive. She kept shaking her hand and even performed CPR while the ambulance were on their way, but nothing worked. James was a very hard sleeper, but even he was awakened by the screams of his pregnant wife while she cried and prayed over her mother.

Within minutes, the ambulance arrived and rushed Mae to the hospital. Although James knew Mable was still a little upset with him, he was there with her the entire time. They waited in the waiting room, but not even 15 minutes later the doctors came out and pronounced her dead. They figured that it was a heart attack, but only the autopsy could determine for sure which would take a few weeks to get back. The one who she confided in and listened to when she needed words of wisdom were now gone and she knew things would never be the same.

Within 48 hours, she found out that she was having twins, had a nasty fight with her husband, and lost her mother. Things seemed like they couldn't get worst for Mable. Although she was pregnant she barely ate anything. She didn't have an appetite and any desire to live. Johnathan and his wife flew in from New York to handle the funeral arrangements. They knew it was too much on Mable to deal with so, they took over. Honestly,

Miracle Bridges

James didn't want Johnathan there regardless of what was going on. Johnathan knew what type of man James really was and wanted nothing to do with him neither. He didn't want his baby sister to be married to him with two more kids on the way, but of course, it was nothing that he could do. Johnathan being more mature than James just stayed focused on the real reason he was there. It was hard for him having to see his only brother, father, and now his mother being buried. Although Johnathan wasn't very religious he knew that the power of life and death was in the hands of God and knew that everything happened for a reason.

His wife Janice was such a sweet lady. She took Mable all around the city. She took her on mini shopping sprees for the babies and took her to get her hair done; something she hadn't ever really done before. They spent a lot of time together that week. Janice and Mable talked several times during the week ont the phone, but being in person together was different especially under the circumstances. Mable really appreciated Janice. Janice made Mable feel more of a woman than James did.

The day of the funeral, James was 30 minutes late and it was totally disrespectful. But, to him 30 minutes late meant that he was on time. The funeral was a bit long. Everyone who was at the funeral only had good things to say about Mae which made Mable and Johnathan feels more at peace. She knew her mother was a motivator, a spiritual leader, a wonderful mom, and she would totally miss her being around.

After the funeral, Mable and Johnathan had a celebration party in their mom's memory instead of a sad memorial. They had all Mae's friends over to the house, even the Pastor and his family came over. They had a huge meal cooked and had dozens of bottles of Sparkling Apple Cider. Apple Cider was Mae's favorite drink. They had tons of fun and nobody really wanted it to end. Mable remembered her mother always saying that when she passed away, she wanted them to smile and not to cry. So, at the party, it was a whole lot of smiling going on. They took pictures and made toasts. Even baby Lacie was in the midst of the party being passed around and getting her little cheeks pinched on. I'm sure she was used to it though because Mae use to do it all the time and Lacie would just giggle.

After the party, Mable and Janice started to clean up while the guys cleaned the yard. It was truly an awesome day for everyone. Even James and Johnathan put their differences aside and had fun. Johnathan came to the realization that if he ever did something wrong and wanted God to forgive him, then he would have to do the same. Although he still didn't like the way James was treating his sister he had to just leave it in God's hands and keep loving him.

After everyone was done they sat on the couch and went through old photo albums. They stumbled over a picture of Mable when she was younger with Mae's high heels on.

Janice laughed and said, "Wow you look just like your mother."

James laughed and said, "You mean her mama." They all laughed.

They always picked on Janice for being so proper, but she was used to it. It was a joke that was part of the family.

They stayed up for about an hour laughing at old photos but then went to bed since Janice and Johnathan had to catch an early flight back to New York.

CHAPTER 3

God Works in a Mysterious Way

One month after Mae's death things seemed like they were going okay. James spent more time at home with Lacie and Mable was finally able to get a break at times and get the rest that she needed. Mable knew that all those times she and Mae had prayed for James were finally being answered. I guess he realized what he was really missing out on. Some nights he would even get up with Mable when she would have contractions and give her massages to ease the pain. She only had a few weeks left until the twins were born. James would make Mable hot chocolate and sit on the couch and rub her stomach. Mable had to admit she never thought this would be happening, but you can never underestimate the power of God. She knew for a fact, that God was working on James inside and out, and she was loving it. She felt like she now had the man that she wanted to marry. James even offered to clean sometimes when she cooked dinner which was a huge thing for him because normally she had to do it all by herself. The last thing Mae said to Mable before she died was don't give up and she didn't. She held on to God's promises and continued to pray for James daily. Mae had the type of faith in God to where you would think he talked to her personally. She used to always tell Mable to listen to that still small voice.

One day, Mable wanted to surprise James by baking him a birthday cake, but little did she know there was a better gift to come for his birthday. When he walked into the house Mable and baby Lacie were sitting at the table with the candles lit on the cake. James walked in and was totally caught off guard. Mable knew James loved cakes baked from scratch so, she refused to spend any money to get instant cake mix.

Besides, he knew the difference in the taste. As she got up to hug him she suddenly felt wet and noticed her water had broken. He didn't know what to do and started to panic. Mable who was already nervous tried to get him to calm down. He got so nervous that he started to pray as he helped her to the car. Mable called her friend to meet her at the hospital to take care of baby Lacie while she delivered the twins. She happily accepted the chance to spend time with little Lacie. It seemed like everyone had been waiting for her to have the twins.

As they rolled Mable to the delivery room she started to tear up thinking about her mom. Wishing that Mae could have been right there beside her like she had been when Lacie was born.

James knew what was going through her mind so he whispered softly in her ear, "Smile Beautiful, it's going to be alright."

That made Mable feel good. James hadn't called her beautiful since they had first gotten married. Thinking that she was going to have the twins as soon as she got there was a disappointment, she found herself still lying there going through contractions and squeezing James hand. He was late getting to the delivery when Lacie was born, but he made sure that it wouldn't happen again.

Two hours later and she could no longer take it. She felt the need to push so, the doctors were called in to see was it time to deliver the twins. Before they were even done fully checking her they saw the head of the first baby coming out. They had to get prepared quickly because ready or not the baby was coming. The first baby girl that came out had a head full of hair and cried loudly. Mable looked at James and saw a tear rolling down his face. He was completely blown away and nervous at the same time. She weighed 6 pounds and 2 ounces. About four minutes later, the other baby girl came out. She wasn't crying at all and was barely breathing. Mable knew that something was wrong when the doctor and nurses rushed in to put her on a breathing machine. Mable tried to ask questions, but they weren't even sure what was going on. Mable grabbed James hand tighter and asked him to pray, and without hesitating, he did so.

Within 20 minutes later, the doctors came in to let them know that both babies were doing fine. They said she only weighed 4 pounds and 1 ounce and that she may have to stay a little longer in the hospital, but everything would be okay. Mable smiled and silently started to thank God. Mable knew that prayer was powerful and that the prayers of the righteous availeth much. As Mable laid there completely exhausted from the entire labor process. James just sat there and watched her sleep. He truly couldn't believe that they were about to welcome two more baby girls into the house. He sat there thinking of names for the girls and thought that Myra and Tyra would be good names for twin girls.

After about an hour passed, Mable woke up and noticed that James was gone. He had snuck out while she was asleep to go see the babies. He was already attached to them and didn't want to let them out of his sight. He tried to sneak back into the room, but Mable was already awake. She still looked tired and was very thirsty so, he requested that they bring her something to drink. They sat there and talked about plans for the babies and he told her about the names he came up with while she was asleep. She agreed that Myra and Tyra were beautiful names for the girls.

When the time came for her to be released from the hospital she was so excited but somewhat disappointed. Tyra was the only one that could come home. Myra had to spend two more days in the hospital to have several tests done on her to make sure that she was okay to be released. When Mable got home she was so surprised about what James did to one of the rooms. She was even more surprised that Johnathan and Janice came in town and helped James decorate the nursery for the twins. When Mable saw Janice, she was so excited. Johnathan was even excited at the fact that he now had two more nieces to spoil.

Although the babies were just born Mable still felt weird not having Myra home with her. Two days seemed like forever before they could pick up Myra, but the time had now arrived. Myra had gained a little more weight which signified that she was doing much better. Mable was so relieved to have both girls at home. Janice had to fly back to New York, but Johnathan stayed for two extra weeks. During that time, so much had happened. James and Johnathan had grown close.

One day she was walking to the kitchen to get the girls a bottle and overheard James apologizing to Johnathan for all the times he hurt Mable and messed around on her. Most women would have gotten mad and went wild, but for some reason, Mable had a wonderful peace about what she was hearing. The Bible said, to confess your sins one to one another and that is what he was doing. God had forgiven him and so did she. Everything was going great and she truly did see a huge change in James. So, she knew his apology was very sincere.

As the guys wrapped up their conversation. She walked in like she hadn't heard anything. They tried to play it off and started talking about the football game that was on. The guys fed the girls while Mable cooked fried fish and fries. The guys loved having hot fish and cold Sprites during a good football game. So, she spoiled them for the night.

Afterwards, she put the girls to sleep and had the rest of the night to

Miracle Bridges

herself. So, she decided to read her Bible for a while. As soon as she opened it her eyes landed on a scripture that said, "If any man be in Christ he is a new creature," which confirmed what she was thinking about when she heard James and Johnathan's conversation. James had mentioned several times in the past that one day he wanted to get baptized, but now when he said it, she knew he was serious about it. That Sabbath when they went to church he decided to give his life to Jesus and finally get baptized. That day was truly special to them both. Mable had never seen James so happy in his life. Mable used to think it was impossible for him to change, but she remembered the type of people God used in the Bible. He used murderers and anyone else who you wouldn't think He could use or even change.

As time went by, the family became close. Mable loved the new changes in James and prayed that it stayed that way.

CHAPTER 4

Times Changes, Lives Changes

Ten years had passed and everything was still going pretty good. The kids were doing great. Lacie played on the girl's basketball team. Myra was a cheerleader and Tyra was an all "A" Honor Roll student. Every time Mable looked at her girls she saw the favor of God on their lives. She sometimes thought if the girls would have been the same if James wouldn't have changed. It's just something that changes inside a child when the dad is present in the home to help raise them. Mable looked at her present situation because in the past she would have never thought James would be the father he was now. But, when God changes a person and they daily surrender to His Will and obey His Word you would surprise how much and how far God can take a person.

James was still working at the shop, but not as much since he was getting older and didn't really have the strength and energy to work on cars like he used to. James used to be able to work on at least 10 to 15 cars a day. Where now, he would only do about 5 to 8 cars a day. The girls had a good relationship with James. He and Myra were inseparable, but when it came to Tyra and Lacie they were always stuck to Mable. James would go to most of the basketball games to see Myra cheer and Lacie play ball. Tyra was always the one that stayed home with her head in the books. When it came time for report cards to come home. Tyra would be the first one to run in and give them her report card. She just knew that she made the honor roll. She studied all the time. The way she studied you would think she was 20 instead of 10. Lacie would pick on her sometimes for being a bookworm, but Tyra didn't care she was proud of herself and nobody was going to make her think anything differently. James was big

Miracle Bridges

on education, so he wanted them all to make all A's. Myra had all B's and 1 C. Lacie had all A's and 2 B's. For some reason, Myra always seemed to fall behind in math. Seeing how proud James were of Tyra getting all A's Myra would feel some type of way about it. She always wanted her dad to be proud of her. James had taken all of them out for ice cream for making good grades in school, but for some reason, Myra felt like she didn't really earn it, she felt that he was just being nice because he didn't want to hurt her feelings, but that wasn't true at all. James was proud of her as well. Myra tried to study like Tyra did, but it just wasn't her. She hated to read, she wanted everything right then. She wanted to make all A's but didn't want to do what it took to get there. Mable noticed something was going on with Myra when she started to avoid her sisters and distance herself. So, Mable asked her one day what was wrong and Myra told her that she just wanted daddy to be proud of her. Mable knew that Myra loved James very much, but she didn't realize that it was that deep to her. Mable being the Christian mother she was, told her that as long as she was trying her best for her Heavenly Father, then her earthly father would always be proud of her.

You see, sometimes we try so hard to please people here on earth. Whether it's our mother, father, sibling, friends, and even sometimes our enemies. It's ok to do your best and succeed at things. But, when you have the wrong motives or think that your good works will get you into Heaven, that's where you mess up at. The Bible said you are saved by faith. We should try less to please people on earth and stop trying to succeed at the goals others set for us. Instead, focused on the plans that God has for us. We will prosper and grow without a doubt. God wants us to be successful. But, He doesn't want it to consume us to where that's all we care about because then that means that being successful becomes our God and God is a jealous God. A lot of people love their car, house, money, education, family, jewelry, clothes, and even food more than they love God. Anything that controls you becomes your God. Even the thing you spend most of your time doing, can easily become your God. They have a saying that says, God first, family second, and everything else will fall into place. Mable lifted up Myra's head and told her that she was beautiful and smart. Most importantly, her dad would always be proud of her. Myra smiled and left the room.

That evening James made it home a little late, so he missed praying with the girls which he always did before they went to bed. However, he still checked on them, but they were sound asleep.

The next morning, the girls got up, ate breakfast, and headed straight for the bus stop. Although they were 15 minutes early they just wanted to wait for it. They were excited because they were having a carnival at their school to raise money for a family who lost their home in a fire. The kids of that family attended that school, so they wanted to show their support by coming up with a creative way to bless them with funds for clothes, food, and other things they needed. The girls saw it as a chance to have fun and couldn't wait to get there.

When they arrived, it was kids everywhere. There were games, food, and all kinds of prizes and they just went crazy. The girls had such a blast that they didn't want to leave when it was time for them to go home. Come to think about it, sometimes Satan gets us to indulge in sin and things that we really desire so deeply that we never want to come home to God and surrender our lives to Him. To give our life over to Jesus Christ so we can live life more abundantly. To experience true peace and joy, not just happiness that can disappear just by a negative situation, but true joy.

When the girls got home they did their daily routine. They did their homework, cleaned up their rooms, ate dinner, and had their family devotion. After everyone was finished, they were to take their baths and prepare for bed. When they were finished, James prayed with the girls before they went to bed and kissed them good night.

Sleeping that night was difficult for Myra. She kept tossing and turning. She was having nightmares about James dying. So, she did what she knew to do and prayed. She prayed so much that she eventually fell asleep praying.

The next morning, while the girls were eating breakfast James noticed that Myra was a little distant. So, he pulled her to the side to see what was going on and she immediately started crying.

He didn't know what to think so he kept saying, "Sweetie what's wrong? What did you do?"

She just looked at him through her beautiful brown eyes and said, "Daddy please don't leave me."

James was shocked by her words as he softly said, "What do you mean Myra? What do you mean Sweetie? Who said I was leaving?"

"Well Daddy, last night I kept having a dream that you died and this angel came to hold me so I would stop crying, but then I woke up. So, Daddy please don't die! Please don't leave me!"

"Listen, Myra I'm not going anywhere, but I must say when it's my time to go it's my time to go. Jesus holds the keys to life and death, so that's not in my control. So, wipe your face and just know that I love you and you will always be my baby girl." Myra wiped her faced and went back to the kitchen to finish her breakfast.

Since James didn't have to go to work until noon, he took the girls to school. Of course, Myra was the last one out of the car. She loved when her daddy took them to school. She hugged his neck and told him she loved him. Myra got out the car and ran to catch up with her sisters. James still smiling from his Myra's comment was feeling like he was on top of the world. He went back to the house and talked to Mable for a little while. He gave her a kissed and went to work as usual. Not knowing that it would be his last kiss. When he got to work, the shop was pretty busy, so he had to get straight to work. He got his tools ready to work on a Chevy Impala which was one of his favorite cars to work on. He was just doing a simple oil change, so it wouldn't take him long at all. James was good at working on cars and could do an oil change with his eyes closed. He was talking as he put the jack under the car and he didn't realize the fatal mistake that he had made. Since customers weren't allowed in the back, it was only him and Mr. Pete. But, Mr. Pete was back and forth between checking in and out the cars and running the cash register. James made sure he had everything he needed before he started the oil change. Not even within minutes, James heard a noise and realized the mistake he made but it was too late, the jack slipped from under the edge of the car and it fell on top of him.

After Mr. Pete took care of the last customer he came to the back to see what the noise was. He kept calling James name, but only to find him trapped under the car and was unresponsive. He quickly jacked of the car and called the ambulance for help. He called Mable to meet them at the hospital.

Mable arrived minutes after the ambulance arrived. She was nervous and didn't know what to expect. She was told several times to wait in the

Miracle Bridges

waiting room. The doctors came out about 25 minutes later and told her that he had lost to much blood and didn't make it. They tried to revive him, but it didn't work. Mable now being weak in the knees and overwhelmed almost fainted, but the doctor was close enough to catch her and transfer her to a chair. She just sat there crying and calling on the Name of Jesus. She didn't know what to do or how to even tell the kids that their father who had just taken them to school five hours ago was now dead.

Her friend that worked only a few blocks down from the hospital came to get her and take her home. She was too weak to drive and could barely focus. All she kept thinking about was how was she going to tell the kids. When the kids got off the school bus they came running in the house. When they saw their mother sitting there with tears dripping down her cheeks they were terrified. They had never seen Mable cry before so they knew something had to be wrong. Mable reached out her arms to welcome them with a hug and asked how their day in school went.

Lacie looked at Mable and asked, "Mommy why are you crying?"

Myra almost knowing what happen asked, "Is it Daddy, Mommy?"

Mable looked at her and gently grabbed her hand and said softly, "Yes Sweetie, Daddy had a little accident at work and he is not coming home anymore."

Tyra trying to process her comment said, "Well, that's okay we can just go to where ever Daddy is to see him."

Mable slightly smiled and said, "One day we will be able to see him again, but Daddy is gone, Sweetie. He had to be rushed to the hospital today and he didn't make it."

As Myra stood there with tears dripping down her cheeks she kept yelling, "I knew! I knew it!"

"Knew what Myra?" Mable asked as she tried to calm her down.

"Last night I kept having a dream about Daddy dying and an angel came to hold me Mommy, but I woke up. Daddy told me this morning he wasn't going anywhere, but now he's gone. I thought he loved us, Mommy?"

Mable hearing those words from her daughter cut like a knife, but she knew she had to say strong.

Lacie replied, "Daddy did love us Myra, but it was his time to go."

"Nothing happens without God's say so. Right Mommy?"

Mable looked at Lacie and said, "Right."

For the next few days, the house was quiet. It just didn't feel right. The only time the girls spoke was when they were having a meal and having devotion. Myra didn't even want to have devotion, neither did she want to pray. James use to pray with the girls before they went to bed and now Myra felt like she couldn't do it alone. Noticing that Myra was taking James lost hard, Mable sat on the porch and talked to her.

"Myra I know it hurts that your father is not here with us, but it's going to be ok. You know your dad loved you very much and if it was up to him he would have stayed here with us forever. But, its a time and a season for everything on earth Sweetie."

Myra looked up at Mable and said, "No Mommy, it's my fault. I had a dream that Daddy died, and he did Mommy."

"Myra Sweetie, it is not your fault. Who knows, you probably had that dream because God wanted you to know what was going to happen. And, the angel was probably in your dream to comfort you and to prepare you for the tragedy that we are now facing. You know Myra in the Bible, God spoke to people through their dreams so maybe He was speaking to you. Besides, He knows that you were close to your father and that you loved him very much. He also knows how you're feeling right now and He will send you peace and comfort. Just hang in there. We are all going through this together, but this too shall pass Sweetie." They sat on the porch a little longer, said a little prayer, and went back in the house.

Mable figured the girls needed some time out. So, the next day she took them for ice cream and to the park. While the kids played at the playground, Mable just reflected on the life that she and James lived together. She felt at peace knowing that James had been baptized and had giving his life to Jesus Christ before he died. It hurt her to think about the way he died though, but knowing that he died doing something that he loved to do which was fixing on cars made her smiled. You know sometimes people die while doing things that love or they die from the consequences of doing the things they love. For instance, if a person loved to drink and got drunk and then they tried to drive home but died in a car accident because they swerved into oncoming traffic. Or if somebody loved fornicating and died from AIDS. Not all things people love to do are pleasing to God. Sin can get some people so caught up in doing the things that they love that they forget the about the things that God loves. And before you know it, their sinful paths have led them to their death. The Bible says that the road of sin leads to death. Also, in Ecclesiates 9:5 it says the dead don't know anything. That's why I never understood when someone dies, someone else says they're in Heaven looking down on you. Even though it may feel comforting, it's not true. When you die, you can't apologize for how you lived or give your life to Jesus then. It will be too late. That's why it's important to live your life in the way God wants you to. Just think about it though, if everyone died and went to Heaven then Jesus dying on the cross would have been pointless and in vain. We must make a choice to die to our flesh daily, and to pick up our cross and follow Him. Mable was at peace and knew that God's Will must be done and was ready to move on with her life.

CHAPTER 5

Time Flies by Fast

Before you knew it the girls were in high school. Mable raised the girls the best way she could without them no longer having a father figure in they're life. Although James death was a hard pill to swallow things had gotten a little easier and she knew it was because of her faith in God. She had truly experienced the strength and joy that God can and will provide for you in your time of need. James had an insurance policy that left more than enough money for the family to be well taken care of.

It was now time for Lacie's graduation and she was excited. She just couldn't stop thanking God for blessing her to graduate. She knew that God cared about every little thing that happened in her life and that when you surrender any issue or task to Him that He would guide you through to success. That day, Mable cried and cried. She couldn't believe that her oldest child was already graduating. Time had truly gone by fast.

That afternoon before Lacie's graduation, Mable spent a lot of time in prayer and the reason being, is that she knew you could teach or raise a child up in a certain way and the next thing you know, they could choose another lifestyle. They could live like they had forgotten everything you ever taught them and fall into the traps of the Enemy. So, she continuously pled the blood of Jesus over her kids.

While Myra and Tyra were at school. Mable decided to take Lacie out to lunch to celebrate her graduating. She more so did it just so they could have some alone time together. Since they were in high school, one on one time was very rare for them to have. It's something about high school that just keeps teenagers busy. Mable offered to take Lacie out who was still stretched out and half sleep in her bed.

One thing about Mable is that she definitely started to take after her mother Mae. She would wake up early in the morning to pray and quietly sing while she got ready for the day. Lacie didn't have to go back to school for the last two days of school. She had already started to enjoy the feeling of not getting up so early in the morning. She got up anyway and got prepared for the day Mable had planned for her. She took a shower and put on the new dress that Mable had bought her. It was a blue dress with a little dash of red in it which were her favorite colors. She sprayed on some perfume and was ready for the day. In less than three hours she would start living her life as an adult and not just the little girl with pigtails that Mable knew her be.

Mable let Lacie drive that day since she had recently gotten her driver license. Mr. Pete had hired a few more workers to work in the shop so he had more than enough time on his hands to do whatever he wanted to do which was teach Lacie how to drive. For some reason, Mr. Pete felt like he was obligated to be there for James family ever since he died. Mable insisted that he didn't have to teach Lacie how to drive and to be honest, she was scared that he would be next to die while driving with Lacie, but he insisted.

As Lacie and Mable got in the car to head to the restaurant Lacie bowed her head and said a silent prayer. Every time Lacie drove she would say a quick prayer before starting the car. It was so amazing that from a young age to growing up into a young adult Lacie loved to pray. Mable smiled at her daughter after she prayed and they pulled off.

About 15 minutes later, they arrived at Taste Buds which was one of the best restaurants in town. It was classy and not very expensive. Plus, they gave you a lot of food for your money. When they walked in they were greeted immediately and were seated shortly after. As the two of them sat their Mable couldn't hold it in anymore. She asked Lacie when was she planning on going to college or what was she thinking about doing after graduating. She asked since she hadn't heard Lacie talking much about what she wanted to do.

Lacie laughed and responded, "Mama I knew that question was coming, but of course, I want to go to college Mama. I was thinking of a junior college and probably work a part-time job here in town so I could be close to you. Just in case I have to, you know come back home." She chuckled.

She knew that Mable would never stop her girls from coming home no matter how old they were. Lacie loved Mable and always wanted to be under her so Mable wasn't surprised by her statement.

Mable looked at her and told her, "Lacie I am so proud of you. You are my oldest child and you are about to experience life as an adult. It's going to be plenty of times where Satan will present an artificial world to you, but don't fall for it. I pray that you remember all that we have taught you. Life as an adult is not easy, but when you place everything in God's hands anything is possible with Him. Also, young lady there will be a lot of guys out there in that college life, so I want you to stay focus on your education because nobody can take your education away from you. Do you hear me?"

"Yes Mam," Lacie replied, "but you don't have to worry about me, Mama. If I didn't learn anything else from you. I learned how to be focused, not to be judgmental, and to hang on to God in any situation. So, I'll be okay, besides dating is not in my plans right now."

Their Pain but God's Promises

The waitress came in time before Lacie and Mable got into a deeper conversation about boys that made her feel uncomfortable. Lacie quickly ordered already knowing what she wanted while Mable on the other hand, couldn't decide. So, Lacie made a suggestion from the pasta selection. Lacie had been there several times with her friends and knew the menu well enough to be a cook there. As they waited for their food Mable went on and on about how proud she was of Lacie.

Sometimes you just have to encourage this younger generation. Some of them probably never heard you've done a good job or I am so proud of you in they're life. The Bible says that life and death is in the power of the tongue which is true. I even read a verse that tells you to lift people up with your words instead of tearing them down. So, there's nothing wrong with encouraging people to keep pushing through life. Sometimes people have a tendency to tear you down with their words because the same things that you're trying to succeed at may be the very thing that they failed at. Some think that if they didn't succeed that you wouldn't or even deserve to succeed. That you shouldn't even waste your time because not being successful in it could lead to heartache. Which in some cases are true, but how will you succeed in something if you never try. Even if you fail at it, it doesn't mean to stop and give up. It just means to try a different approach or observe where you went wrong at and try again. The Bible tells us that a righteous man may fall seven times, but he will rise again. That is more than enough encouragement for me to keep pushing through life no matter how many times you have failed. So, how about you? God wants us to succeed in life, but if succeeding in something will make us big headed and prideful to the point where we think that we don't need Him anymore, then we have a problem on our hands.

The waitress came out in no time bringing them their food. Everything smelt good and really boosted their appetite. Mable couldn't believe how much pasta they put on her plate. She had enough to take home to the girls and still be full. They sat there for about an hour just enjoying their quality time together. After they finished, they got boxes for their leftover food and headed back home.

The next day, Lacie anxiously prepared for graduation. She put on her cap and gown and kept looking in the mirror smiling. She soon took it off since graduation was four hours away. Whether or not she knew what life would bring as an adult she felt like she could take the world by storm. Lacie wasn't like most teenagers graduating college though. Some teenagers say that they couldn't wait to get out of their parents' house so that they could do what they wanted without nobody telling them what to do. My aunt use to tell me that a hard head makes a sore tail and until this day I live by that saying. Lacie actually didn't want to leave home, she wanted to stay close to Mable for the rest of her life if she could.

Mable picked up the girls early from school to spend time with Lacie before her graduation. They were called to the office and they knew why. They came running full speed to the car looking forward to their day. The girls talked and laughed the entire time.

When Lacie arrived at the school she had to go meet with the other graduates for instructions. While they waited in the auditorium for the program to start, Myra and Tyra just went on and on about how they couldn't wait to graduate themselves. I think seeing love and support from family and friends had motivated them to finish school. They were going to be juniors next year and felt like it was going by very slow.

Within 20 minutes, the program started. They talked for a least 30

Their Pain but God's Promises

minutes before started calling the names of the graduates. When they called Lacie's name she bowed and blew kisses to the crowd showing her silly side. Grabbed her diploma and walked off the stage while her sisters continued to scream her name and clap loudly.

After the graduation, everyone met out front to wait for the graduates. People were everywhere, and kids were running wild. When Lacie finally came out they took a few pictures and got in the car to go home. She didn't really want to go to the graduation parties that people were having, she just wanted to celebrate with her sisters.

When they pulled up at home they noticed a strange car in the yard. Mable made them stay in the car while she went to see who it was, but before she got to the window Mr. Pete opened the car door and got out with a huge smile on his face holding a set of car keys in his hand.

He walked up to Mable's car and opened the front door to let Lacie out and said, "This car is not going to drive itself." She looked at Mable with a surprised look her on her face and quickly got out to hug Mr. Pete.

"I think you deserve to have your own car now," replied Mr. Pete, "just drive the way I taught you and you should be alright."

Lacie kept saying thank you, thank you, thank you, Mr. Pete, while motioning for her sisters to get out the car and go for a spin. They bolted out the car trying to see who could make it to the front seat. They always raced for the front seat, no matter who vehicle it was. Lacie loved her car! It was a little Honda Civic, but it was hers. As the girls got in the car Lacie made sure that they had their seat belt on and said her prayer as she always did before she drove anywhere. She felt like she was on top of the world. She had just graduated and now she had a new car. The girls turned on some 'Mary Mary' as loud the radio could go and went rolling down the street.

Mable looked at Mr. Pete and thanked him for all he had done for them. He simply said thank you and told her that James was such a huge blessing to him at the shop when they were working together. And that he just wanted to be a blessing to the girls in whatever way he could. Although Mr. Pete always gossiped about people, he still had a kind heart and Mable really appreciated that about him. Mr. Pete knew that when God blessed you, that you should be a blessing to others, that way more blessings will come your way. He truly did have a heart for helping people though. He gave Mable a hug and got in his car and left.

Mable waited on the porch until the girls got back. Meanwhile, she kept thinking about how good the Lord is. She couldn't help thinking about how He has brought her family a long way. Her mother was dead, her brother was dead, her father was dead, as well as her husband, but she still knew that her Heavenly Father was alive and well.

Her oldest brother Johnathan and her sister-in-law Janice had moved to California so she didn't see them as much as she used to, but they often kept in touch over the phone. Myra wasn't too impressed about California so during some of the summers she turned down the invitation to visit. As for Lacie, she was going to stay at home of course, so she could be under Mable. Tyra, on the other hand, loved California and every chance she got to go there she went. Sometimes she didn't even want to come home. It was something about California that made her feel like she just fit in.

Just when Mable was about to stand up, the girls pulled up and hopped out of car talking about how cool the car was. They went in the house and spent all night playing games, eating ice cream and cake, and watching movies. Lacie enjoyed being with her sisters instead of being at someone's party where she felt uncomfortable. Lacie was an outgoing girl but wasn't the party type. She was the person that some of the other students came to if they had a problem and needed someone to talk to. Lacie had a welcoming Spirit about her that made people feel completely comfortable. That's why it wasn't surprising that she wanted to major in Psychology. Sometimes in order to find out what our purpose is, we must look at gifts that God has giving us, which more than likely is the field that we should be working in. For an example, if God gave you the ability to have a high tolerance for people and a good personality then maybe some type of customer service would be a good job for you. If someone was good at math then maybe a job in Marketing or Accounting would be a good job for them. Not everyone is destined to be a singer or an actress.

As the girls continued to have fun they realized that it was almost 2 in the morning. Mable had been asleep since 10 pm and the girls were still awake and fully energized but figured that they should quiet down and get some sleep.

CHAPTER 6

Pressure and Pain

That week, Lacie spent a lot of time sending trying to find a college that was right for her. She was soon accepted at J.O.U. Junior College. It was an awesome school and they had a lot of Christian based courses. Mable was happy for her because that was a college that she really wanted to go to and her financial aid paid for everything. Lacie wanted to get her associates degree in Psychology and work part-time. She got a part-time job working at a juvenile detention center. They hired her as the Activities Coordinator because she was majoring in Psychology and had an outgoing personality. So, they were confident that she could handle the job.

As time went by, she started to get more hours at work and started to spend less time at school. Her grades were starting to slip and it was really too much to bear, but she insisted on pushing on. Mable tried to encourage her to focus more on school though. Lacie continued to work but told Mable that she would work on getting her grades up so she wouldn't lose her financial aid.

Tyra and Myra were now seniors in high school and was enjoying the senior life. They kept in their minds if they could make it through the rest of the year that they would soon be graduating. When it was time for the senior prom, Tyra was excited, but Myra really wasn't. For one, she didn't have anyone to go with and two, she just simply didn't want to go. Lacie insisted that she go since she didn't go to her junior prom.

Lacie helped the girls find the perfect dress and thought that maybe it was a good idea for Myra to go out with one of the guys from the juvenile detention center named Cedrick, he and Myra were the same age. Cedrick had only ended up in the detention center because he and his friends got into a little mischief and got into a few fights, so it wasn't anything major. Lacie had worked with him ever since he had arrived at the detention center and she felt like he was a good kid. He would help her clean and put up the games when most of the kids just left it messy and did whatever they wanted to do. Of course, Lacie had to get it cleared with her supervisors before giving Myra the green light. They had no reason to doubt Lacie's judgment towards Cedrick and they decided to let him go. Myra took Lacie's advice and agreed to go. Tyra was going with this guy from her third period English class who she thought was hilarious. He was a very popular guy in school, so she was honored to go with him. Tyra had always been the smart one, but now she had the brains and the beauty that everyone noticed. Being twins you would have thought Tyra and Myra acted the same, looked the same, and did everything the same. They were close indeed, but Myra wasn't as outgoing as Tyra was. Myra no longer had the desire to cheer as she did in elementary and middle school. She changed a lot since James died and it still affects her until this day.

Lacie took the girls to the salon to get their hair done since Mable wasn't feeling too well. They spent about four hours getting their hair and nails done. They made sure that everything was set in place for the prom that night.

Lacie called her supervisor to see if there was anything Cedrick needed. Cedrick was really excited about going to the prom because he had never gotten a chance to experience it for himself and now he had his chance.

The girls went to the house to start getting ready for the prom. Tyra's dress was a pinkish color with a little white in it. It had glittery stones on it as well. Myra's dress was even more beautiful. Her dress was blue and black with silver streaks that were breathtaking at the sight of it. Mable spent at least 20 minutes taking pictures of the girls before it was time for them to leave. Lacie let Myra drive her car to the prom even though she knew the girls didn't have their driver license yet, but she took that risk. Besides, it was their senior prom and they didn't want anyone dropping them off or picking them up other than a Limo.

Tyra's date was a little late getting there, but when he got there Mable took even more pictures. Cedrick was already there. Lacie's supervisor dropped him off at Mable's house so he and Myra could ride together. Myra gave Lacie and Mable a hug and her and Cedrick left for the prom. He was amazed at how beautiful Myra looked and was excited to be seen with her. When they arrived at the school there were cars everywhere so finding a place to park was very difficult. They had to park in the third parking lot which was halfway around the building. Since other people had to walk it wasn't that bad. As they were walking from the parking lot, Myra ran into several people she knew that gave her compliments on how cute she looked because this was a totally different image of what they usually saw at school. Hearing all the compliments that they gave Myra made Cedrick like her even more.

About 15 minutes later, Tyra and her date showed up. The music was loud, everyone was dancing and having a good time. There was so much food. They had the tables covered with different types of food and mixed fruit drinks. The lights were beautiful and Myra realized it was as good as Lacie said it was. They took more pictures at the prom.

Myra was a good dancer, especially counting that she was a cheerleader for four years throughout elementary and middle school also.

On top of that, she was a flag girl for a year in high school. Tyra didn't have much rhythm, but that didn't stop her from having fun. They danced and laughed so much until they were nearly out of breath. The prom drew Myra and Tyra even closer and they didn't want the night to end.

After the prom was over a lot of people hung outside and talked about what had happened during the prom and how much fun they had. Myra introduced Cedrick to a few of her friends and they seemed to like him. Since he had never experienced prom before it was a night that he would never forget. Tyra and her friends talked about going to eat at Taste Buds, so everyone agreed to go. When they arrived at the restaurant it was completely packed. It took them at least 20 minutes before they even got seated, but they didn't care because they were still filled with adrenaline from all the fun they had just had. They were seated at their tables and ordered their drinks. They tried to wait for more of their friends to show up, but they went ahead and ordered they're food. It came out about 25 minutes later and they talked more and laughed more and ate off each other plates. Everyone ordered something different just so they could eat off each other plates. Myra must have eaten the wrong thing because her stomach wasn't feeling too well. She drank a Sprite to see if it would make her feel better, but it didn't. Not wanting to ruin everyone's fun, she decided that she and Cedrick were just going to leave. She grabbed the keys and headed for the door.

As soon as she made it to the car she threw up almost everything she had eaten. Cedrick rushed to her side of the car and rubbed her back as she kept vomiting. Myra apologized, feeling really embarrassed and motioned to him that she was ok. He insisted that she let him drive and lied saying that Lacie had let him drive once before to pick up things for activities.

She believed him and gave him the keys. They drove for a little while.

Myra noticed that he missed his turn, so she softly said, "I think you just missed the turn."

He told her that he wanted to stop by a corner store to grabbed a few things because once he got back to the detention center he wouldn't be able to go out, so she agreed that it was okay. For some reason, there were starting to be less and less lights so Myra suggested that they turn back around before they got lost. She had been by Lacie's job before and never been the way that they were going. But before she knew it, he had stopped the car and turned to look at her.

He grabbed her hand and said, "Myra I know you don't really want me to go back to the detention center just yet. So, don't play hard to get."

She confusingly looked at him and said, "Yes I do want you to go back. I'm not feeling well and I don't want you to get in trouble just because you got back too late. You are supposed to be back in by 2 am and it's already 1:38 am."

"Yeah, your right Myra, but we have a little time to spend together."

He tried to make a pass at her, but she moved her head which made Cedrick furious. He grabbed her face forcing her to kiss him. She was already weak from being nauseated so she couldn't put up much of a fight. He pushed her back against the passenger seat causing her to hit her head against the window and she passed out. He lifted up her skirt and did all sorts of things to her until a man knocked on the window. The man shined a flashlight into the car and saw what was going on. Being in trouble many times before, Cedrick tried to come up with an excuse for what was going on. He lied and said that he and his girlfriend were making out and she went to sleep which didn't seem to make sense to the man. The man was actually an off-duty police officer and he felt something iffy was going on so he called for back up, just in case. Little did Cedrick know that it was an arsenal only two miles away. Knowing that he was in some serious trouble he kept saying just let us leave so I can take my girlfriend home we have a curfew. But, the off-duty officer refused to let them leave.

The police arrived within 5 minutes and asked Cedrick for his license and registration. When he gave them the registration and insurance to the car, but couldn't provide his license, the officer knew it was something going on indeed. When the other cop saw that Myra was unresponsive he called for an ambulance. He wrote down Cedrick's social security number and ran his information. What came up in the computer was completely shocking. The little mischief that Lacie's thought he did that landed him in the detention center appeared to be a lot more. He also had a rape case that was sealed up, but still showed in the system. The officer looked at the info on the insurance card and called Lacie right away.

"Excuse me Mam, my name is Officer Davis and we have your car. Do you know a Cedrick Thomas?"

Lacie on the other line nervously said, "Yes Sir. What's wrong?"

"Well, Mam an off-duty officer noticed your car suspiciously park in a 'No Trespassing Zone' and found Mr. Thomas in your car with a young lady that appears to be unconscious. It seems as if a rape took place, but we wouldn't know for sure until she is admitted to the hospital. They will be taking her to Parker Stone Hospital. Without hearing anything more, Lacie woke Mable up and they rushed to the hospital.

When they arrived there, they were directed to room 203 where Myra had been admitted. She had just awakened and had a bruise on the side of her head where she hit the window. A few scratches, but nothing major.

However mentally she was destroyed. When Myra saw Lacie's face she instantly started crying and asked Lacie why did she allow that to happen to her. That she didn't even want to go to the prom, but she pressured her to go.

Lacie replied, "Myra I didn't know, I'm so sorry." She tried to grab Myra's hand, but she snatched it away.

"Don't touch me, Lacie. You work with Cedrick every day and you didn't know that he would do something like this to me. The police said that he raped someone before, but the case was sealed. How did you not know? How could you Lacie? How could you not know?"

The truth is, that Lacie really didn't know, it was some things the company couldn't speak about because of legal purposes. It was respecting other people's privacy and safety. She tried to tell Myra that she didn't know and that she was sorry, but Myra was extremely outraged and hurt to hear her or even look at Lacie.

Tyra sat there beside Myra and shook her head saying, "Lacie just give her some space, she doesn't need to be upset right now."

Lacie looked at Mable. Mable handed Lacie the keys, so she could take her car and she walked out of the door. On her way out of the hospital she just kept saying, "God forgive me I didn't know." She cried and prayed out loud to herself. She really felt bad for what had happened. She knew that ever since their dad died that trusting or getting close to anyone was hard for Myra.

She asked two of her friends to meet her at the police station to pick up the car. She needed someone to drive Mable's car back to the hospital. When she walked into the police station Cedrick was still sitting there in handcuffs waiting to be booked in. Myra made it clear that she wanted

Mable to press charges on him and because he was about to turn 18 in 3 days so he would be tried as an adult. Cedrick looked up and saw Lacie looking at him.

"How could you Cedrick? I trusted you. I thought you were this innocent boy who only got in trouble a few times and regretted doing what he did. I gave you a chance to prove yourself, that you weren't what people said you were and you proved me wrong. You hurt my sister and you hurt me. Now because of what you did, she doesn't even want me in her presence, our precious relationship is ruined because of you! May God have Mercy on your Soul!"

He just put his head down feeling every word that was just spoken to him. He knew he messed up and that his life was never going to be the same again. Lacie walked up to the counter to fill out the paperwork to get her car released back to her. It didn't take much time before the process was done and her keys were now back in her possession. On the way out the door, Cedrick called Lacie's name.

Not wanting to talk to him she turned around and looked at him as he sincerely said to her, "I'm sorry. I never meant to hurt you. I know I messed up and I pray that God will forgive me as well as your family."

Lacie thinking back to the scripture that says forgive those who sinned against you and your Father in Heaven will also forgive you. She looked at him and said apology accepted and walked out the door. Lacie knew that to hold on to a grudge or unforgiveness could have you in emotional and spiritual bondage and she didn't want to experience that. It hurt her deeply indeed for what Cedrick had done, but she knew that God would take care of it and that he would reap what he sowed.

Lacie gave her mother's car keys to her friend so she could trail behind her to the hospital. When they arrived, Myra was sleeping and Tyra was downstairs at the cafe that stayed open 24 hrs. Mable came outside the door not wanting to wake Myra up.

As Mable closed the door to the room to talk to Lacie she saw the sadness in Lacie's eyes and said, "It's going to be alright Lacie. I know you had no idea about that boy and would never put your sisters in harms ways. Things may seem a little crazy now, but this too shall pass." Lacie gave Mable a kiss and turned away to leave.

That night Lacie just kept replaying in her head everything that happened, but most of all she was thinking about the once precious relationship that she and Myra had was now broken and only God could mend it.

CHAPTER 7

Time of Trouble

Myra was released from the hospital the next day and went home. Things were a little weird for her. Kids at school found out what had happened and some even had the nerve to make fun of her. It hurt her deeply to the point where she didn't even want to go to school anymore. Although it was only four more months left of school she couldn't bare going there every day to take the torment. She decided to drop out while Tyra continued to go to school and eventually graduated. Tyra applied for a college in California at CAU and received a full scholarship. She felt bad about leaving Myra, but she knew she had to prepare herself for the real world. She promised to always keep in contact with her though.

Tyra had to fly out in a few weeks after being accepted into CAU. The semester was starting soon and she wanted to jump head first in school. She knew the longer she stayed with Myra the harder it would be for her to go. Tyra stayed with Johnathan and Janice for her first two years of college, but then they helped her get her own apartment. Meanwhile, Myra stayed at home with Mable and worked hard to get her GED. Sometimes Myra regretted dropping out, but she couldn't bear the pain of being called almost everything you could think of. And being looked down on when what had happened wasn't her fault at all. One thing she failed to realize was that they even talked about Jesus when he walked this earth, but he continued to push on and was always about His Father's business.

Myra had started to change even more. The way she talked, her attitude, her ambition, and even her spiritual life. She no longer wanted to pray with Mable like she used to. And every time Lacie came by the house to pick Mable up for church she would pretend to be asleep. Myra would hang out until about 3 in the morning. She was hanging out with people who had totally different morals than she did, but she no longer cared. She figured that she had one life and she was going to live it. She had this mindset of only God could judge her which was true, but how He was going to judge her is what was important. We are not talking about somebody who is living like a heathen, that never knew the Word of God. Myra was indeed raised up in a Christian home and knew the power that God had, but suddenly didn't want anything to do with Him.

Years went by and her behavior had gotten worst. Tyra was doing great in California and Lacie had finally obtained her degree in Psychology. Even though she dropped classes and made low grades, she found the time, knowledge, and strength to pull her grades back up. That's one thing she realized, that no matter how old you are, you still have a purpose and that you're never too old to learn something new or go back to school.

Myra ended up moving out of Mable's house and moving into a one-bedroom apartment with a guy that she barely knew. He was known around town and wasn't known for anything good. Myra thought she was grown and was determined to make something out of herself by any means necessary. Lacie would come over Mable's house almost every day to make sure she had breakfast and dinner or whatever else she needed. Mable was a little sick and never did tell the girls what was wrong with her. Every time someone asked her how she was doing she would say alright. On the outside, Mable may have looked alright, but on the inside, she was hurting because of her broken family and she wanted to get that back. But, were the relationships with her daughters too much to mend?

Was the family really broken to the point where it was impossible for them to be like they use to be? Their lives were indeed different. As a matter of fact, I will take you through each one of their lives so you can see for yourself.

CHAPTER 8 - PART 1 TYRA

Separated and Different

Tyra was still living in California, she seemed to have everything she needed. She had graduated from CAU with her Master's degree in Business Administration and had a full-time job as a realtor. She sold houses from left to right and was very good. Tyra would call Mable occasionally to see how she was doing. Each time she called Mable told her that she was doing fine, so she figured there was no need to keep calling her every day asking her the same questions. All they really talked about was Tyra most of the time anyway.

Tyra had changed a lot, she had become a successful business major/realtor that acted like she owned the world and everyone in it. Where did she get pride and boasting from? Beats Mable. She taught her girls to be confident in themselves, but Tyra was way passed being confident. She was arrogant, conceited, and she didn't even date anymore. Whenever she did, she intimidated the men for not making as much money as she did and she felt that she was wasting her time anyway. Besides, she had everything she wanted, so a man would just be getting in the way of things.

One time this guy tried to take her out on a date to a restaurant. He wanted to wine and dine her; he wanted to show her a good time. Everything was going well until the owner of the restaurant came out to the table and started talking to her date. Come to find out, they were roommates back in college. So, the owner of the restaurant offered him a management position if he ever wanted to come work with him. He told him that he would think about it which made Tyra sick to her stomach. Although he was just a blue-collar worker he asked for Tyra's opinion about it.

When they left the restaurant she chewed him out.

Making the situation more than what it was, she started saying all kinds of things like, "You can't take care of me, Sweetie you didn't even pay the bill. The owner of the restaurant did and besides, why would you even want to work in a restaurant and better yet, work for someone else?"

He interrupted her lame opinions and said, "Tyra, I may not make more money than you or have a bigger house, but what I do have, I've worked hard for it. I'm not out on the corner trying to sell nickel and dime drugs. I am a man who works honestly to get what I need in life. So, if that's not enough for you then maybe you should look for someone else."

About 15 minutes later, he arrived in front of her house without having anything else to say to her. So, Tyra looked at him and said, "Well bye."

When she got out of the car, she looked back at him, and made motions with her hands for him to go away like he was some type of stray dog or something. He drove off without second-guessing himself or looking back. Tyra was cold-hearted towards men and didn't really care. She couldn't keep a man in her life because of all the boasting and bragging she did; as if she had it all together. The Bible says, to put your riches away in Heaven and not on earth where thieves can destroy, but she did just the opposite.

Tyra only liked two guys in her lifetime. One was Edward Jones which was the same guy who took her to her junior and senior prom. They had dated for a short period after they graduated high school. However, she was focused more on her career, so she broke up with him, went to California, and started going to college. He didn't worry about it, but he was hurt. He knew that if it was meant for them to be together then nobody could stop it from happening.

The other guy she liked was Daniel Logan. He was a drum major in the college band and majored in Criminal Justice. He had cousins in the music industry which was one of the reasons Tyra was interested in him. He was well-known around campus, but he was known for the wrong things. He was a total party animal, but she figured maybe if they dated long enough she could change him into the man she wanted him to be. That's the problem, nobody can change a person that doesn't want to change. You can do all you can for that person, but if they're not ready to change or fully surrender to God then change will never take place. But, she would learn the hard way.

One night after a college game, he invited Tyra to one of his cousin's parties. She wasn't the party type, but she went anyway. Tyra had never drank alcohol or did any kind of drugs a day in her life. A lot of the guys at the party were acting crazy and drinking like thirsty deers at a spring. Daniel tried to help her get a little comfortable, but it just wasn't something that Tyra was used to. There were a lot of other girls there that were acting crazier than the guys.

Tyra thought that she would excuse herself and step outside to get some air. She stayed outside for a little while just to get away from all the smoking and everything else that was going on. The music was loud, but no one seemed to care. They just continued to laugh loudly and party like rock stars. Tyra felt very uncomfortable because she was around people that were engaging in the same things that Mable warned her about. It's interesting how parents teach their children certain morals and raise them up in a church environment, and then they just totally go astray, but she didn't in this case. Satan has a way to put stumbling blocks in people's way. And when we are not wrapped up in the Word of God and dying to our flesh daily it's easy to fall for it.

Tyra turned around to go back inside the house, but was blocked by two of Daniel's friends. They tried to corner her saying all type of things like, girl you look good, what's up with us, and all types of foolish things. Daniel was watching the whole scene, so she looked at him thinking that he was going to say something. But, all he said was, "If you're down for it, go for it." Tyra looked at him in disbelief because she thought that they were actually dating. Now hearing him give her the go-ahead to sleep with his friends was very disrespectful to her. The two guys just looked at her as another girl walked up to Daniel and kissed him on the cheek. Tyra felt hurt and played. She turned around to head to her car while the guys just kept saying how stuck-up she was. She totally ignored them and went on her way. She had really liked Daniel but found out that everything that looked good wasn't good.

That's where a lot of people go wrong. They look at what a person has in their bank account, what kind of car they drive, where they live, what size house they live in, and what type of people they hang around. And get caught totally off guard by all the unnecessary baggage that they have. That's why it is so important to get to know a person for who they really are and not for what they have or what they can give you. Money can buy happiness, but it can't buy joy. A lot of people think happiness and joy is the same thing when it's not. Happiness comes from certain situations and achievements while joy comes from the Lord. When you have joy, it doesn't matter what situation tries to devastate you, because you will still smile and trust God. You can be completely broken from past hurts and have not a dime to your name, but still feel peace and nobody can take that away or buy that feeling.

Miracle Bridges

Tyra got in her car and left. From that day on, she made up in her mind that she was going to be ruthless to men no matter what. She figured that all guys were the same and didn't want anything, but sex. Any guy after that incident with Daniel that wanted to take her out on a date was deeply humiliated and kicked to the curb. Don't get me wrong, Tyra wanted to be loved, but guys had to measure up to her standards and nothing less. The rate that Tyra was going, it would be impossible for her to find true love. After a while, she had gotten into a habit of not dating at all. She was just focused on building her business.

Johnathan and Janice flew out a few times to visit Mable in Tennessee and tried to encourage Tyra to go, but she refused. She figured her business was more important and that she just didn't have time for traveling at the moment. Although she would send gifts and cards to make-up for not being there, it still didn't do any good. Well, at least to Mable it didn't. Myra loved the gifts and looked forward to getting them whenever Tyra didn't come to visit. Tyra spoiled Myra like she was a little child and it was ridiculous.

They say you can give a man a fish and he will eat for a day, but if you teach a man how to fish, he can eat for a lifetime. That is a very true statement indeed. Sometimes we try to help people so much and do so much for them that we make them disabled. We actually take away their independence. They forget how to do things for themselves and eventually don't even want to do things for themselves because they expect you to do it for them.

Tyra had all the money her heart could desire, but without love, she had nothing.

PART 2

Myra

Myra was still staying with her so-called boyfriend. She lived about 20 minutes away from Mable. She would see Lacie from time-to-time and sometimes wouldn't even speak to her. She still held a grudge against her for what happened to her on her prom night. The word was that Cedrick would only had to do four years and would soon be released from jail.

Myra's life was a hot mess. After she moved out of Mable's house and moved in with DJ. She would come back from time-to-time when Johnathan and Janice visited to get the gifts Tyra had sent. At first, Myra's boyfriend seemed like a nice guy. He took good care of Myra for the first few months that they were together. She loved DJ and would do anything for him. He bought her clothes and all type of unnecessary things that she didn't need, but things changed rather quickly.

One night, Myra went out to celebrate with her girlfriends because one of them had just gotten engaged. When she got back home, DJ was sitting on the couch in the dark. He scared her half to death when she turned on the lights. He was staring at her with this devilish look on his face.

Then he asked her, "Where have you been Myra? I've been sitting here waiting for you."

"Sweetie you couldn't have been waiting for me that long. It's only 11:05 pm and I said that I would be home at 11."

He stood up and walked over to her and said, "Exactly, it's 11:05 you're five minutes late. Don't ever have me waiting for you again! Who do you think you are?"

She couldn't believe how insane he was acting over her being 5 minutes late, so she turned around to walk to the bedroom. He grabbed her arm and smacked her in the face causing her to fall to the floor. She looked at him and was in shock that he had just hit her. He realized what he had done and immediately started apologizing to her. She knew that a man was never supposed to hit a woman, especially a woman he loved. So, she thought that maybe it was something that was done out of anger and that he was sincerely sorry for what he did. He picked her up and hugged her. He told her that he was sorry and she fell for it. They went over and sat on the couch. That's when she noticed a tray laying there with a white powdery substance on it. Now it made sense to her that maybe he was high. Maybe he couldn't control his temper and accidentally hit her. She was making up all kinds of excuses for his irrational behavior. DJ grabbed the straw that was on the tray and proceeded to sniff a line of the powdery substance that Myra later found out was cocaine. He looked her in the eyes and asked her if she loved him.

She replied, "Of course I do DJ."

He told her that if she loved him and always wanted to be with him that they needed to be on one accord. He motioned for her to take the straw from his hand and do the same thing that he just did. She started to hesitate because the only drugs she ever had was alcohol. She looked at him before proceeding and as she did, a tear dropped down her cheek because she knew she was doing the wrong thing. She knew her mom had always taught them not to do drugs and to stay away from anyone who did.

He sat back on the couch and smiled at the fact that he had her wrapped around his finger. That night, Myra just laid there. She was so high that she didn't know what to do. She was afraid and just laid in the bed wondering where she had gone wrong. Little did she know, her life was going to take a turn for the worst.

Since he no longer had to hide the fact that he was doing drugs; he would send her to buy them or have the drug man come to the house. From time-to-time, it would be different guys, but they all made plays for the same person.

One night around 8 o' clock, Myra had come home from shopping. Tyra had sent her some money because Myra didn't have a job at the time. Besides, her twin sister had money on top of money, so she didn't mind asking her for some.

When she walked into the house, one of the drug dealers had just gotten there. Myra decided to head to the back in order to give them some privacy. DJ called Myra back into the living room because he was short about $25. He needed her to pay the rest, but she had spent it all on shopping and only had $12 left. DJ knew Myra had money because he found the Western Union receipt from Tyra for $500. He was mad that Myra went out and blew $500 like it was nothing. So, he had agreed to pay the dude back on that following Friday with interest, but he refused the I Owe You deal that DJ offered him. Money wasn't an issue for these guys and neither was women, but he thought that Myra was very pretty and saw this as an opportunity to get exactly what he wanted. He asked to speak with DJ in private, so DJ made Myra leave the room as the two of them talked. DJ already knew what he wanted and figured that since Myra was his property, he could do whatever he wanted with and to her. Plus, Myra was scared of DJ, so it wouldn't be that hard to get her to do whatever he wanted. DJ called Myra in the living room and told her what she had to do to pay the debt. She started crying because she thought that

DJ really loved her. Also, what he was asking from her was very disrespectful. She didn't want to do it, but she knew the consequences if she didn't. Besides, at this point, she was hooked on cocaine and used it at least three times a day. As degraded as she felt, she took him to the back room and performed her sexual duties in exchange for the drugs.

As time went by, her sleeping with guys to pay off the debt for drugs became a regular thing. She had gotten use to it. DJ no longer was her boyfriend but was more like her pimp. Myra knew she was falling deeper into sin and felt that getting up was impossible. She prayed to get cleaned and delivered from drugs, but she kept falling into temptation.

What she failed to realize was that in order to fully change her ways, she had to separate herself from people who were indulging in the same things that she was battling with. Myra was going through a serious Spiritual warfare. Demons were attacking her and getting in her head. They were telling her that she was never going to be anybody and that she needed DJ to love her because no one else would. Myra had sunken low to the point where she wasn't just doing cocaine, but she was also popping pills. DJ introduced Myra to this guy name Cortez. He had his own pornography business and wanted Myra to work with his company. He offered her $3,000 for every movie she did. She had agreed because she knew that she needed the money to supply her drug habit. Myra didn't mind working for him since she was already doing that type of work and wasn't getting as much money for it. Myra knew about sexual sins and how her body was a temple, but she was enticed by the money and drugs. Therefore, that thought went out the window.

Erin was the guy who did the recording and he really liked Myra. When he looked at her, he didn't see a porn star. He saw a woman who was broken and needed love, so he took an interest in getting to know her.

A few weeks went by, and other people didn't think much about them being too close, they just thought it was business. DJ didn't care either. All he cared about was her making money to support their drug habits. As Myra and Erin spent more time together she noticed that she was slowly getting off drugs. They would do things that she always wanted to do. They would go to carnivals, go bowling, take pictures, and sometimes even went out for ice cream whenever they had the time. It reminded her of when James would take her and her sisters out for ice cream.

As Erin and Myra grew closer, he started to ask her more about her family and what her childhood was like. She opened up to him a little, but still left out a lot of the details. She eventually introduced him to Mable and even Lacie once. Lacie knew the type of lifestyle Myra was living but refused to talk about it with her. She just kept praying for her sister and enjoyed the fact that Myra had even spoken a few words to her.

Three months later, Myra found out that she was pregnant by Erin and didn't know what to do. Although Erin worked in the pornography business he knew that it was still wrong to fornicate. He started to feel a heavy conviction and left the company. The only reason he took the job in the first place was because Cortez was his first cousin. Also, he had fallen on hard times, so he accepted Cortez's job offer. Erin and Myra came up with all kinds of ideas to deal with her pregnancy. Myra wanted to have an abortion and just get it over with. She wasn't ready to be a mom and didn't know how to be a mom. However, Erin didn't believe in taking an innocent life. Myra was still in her relationship with DJ, but she had feelings for Erin and didn't know how to handle the situation. Myra had really slowed down on doing drugs, but DJ didn't care because it was more for him and she was still bringing the money to the table.

After considering different options for about a week, Erin talked Myra into moving with him to Orlando Florida. Although Myra agreed to move, she continued to pressure Erin into letting her have an abortion, but he refused to do that. He knew that the baby wasn't a sin, but the act of fornication that created the baby was a sin. Myra was not ready to be a mother at all. She pleaded and pleaded with him until they finally made a decision. The decision was that Myra would have the baby, sign over full custody to him, and then return to Tennessee.

During the time of Myra's pregnancy, a change started happening in Erin. He knew he had screwed up. He knew that all the lies and deceit was wrong. He knew that fornication was wrong and that God didn't approve of it. He started to seek counseling and asking God to take control of the situation. When it was time for Myra to have the baby, Erin was right by her side. They had a baby boy and named him Erin Jr., so nobody would figure out it was her child. Just as they had planned, she signed over all her legal rights to Erin and returned to Tennessee. Of course, Erin was hurt, but he knew the deal that they made and it wasn't going to change. He had hoped that she would change her mind, but she didn't. So, he figured that he would just continue to pray for her. After all, he loved Myra and she was the mother of his only child. Erin was going to go back to Tennessee but decided to stay in Florida for few years so that everything would fall into place and wouldn't raise suspicion. He figured if he stayed in Florida for a few years and came back to Tennessee with a child that people would assume that either he and his wife separated or that she had left him to care for their son. However, it's said that what's done in the dark will always come to the light, but was it true in this case?

PART 3

Lacie

A few years after Lacie had gotten her degree in Psychology she had begun working at an elementary school as a counselor. She had been there for five years and felt like that's where God wanted her to be. She realized that some things that kids needed to talk about at school were impossible for them to talk about at home. Some of the reasons are that some parents never seem to have time to talk or that some kids don't feel comfortable talking to their parents about certain things. Also, in some cases, they are being abused at home. Whether it's mentally or physically, they always seemed comfortable talking to Lacie.

When Lacie wasn't working, she was at Mable's house cooking and cleaning. Lacie's life didn't consist of much and she didn't mind. She had always been close to Mable. Maybe that was something the kids picked up on about Lacie and probably wanted to have someone to love them, like the way she loved Mable. Lacie truly loved the kids. Sometimes she would get permission from some of the parents to take students to the park after school. She would sometimes stop by the store and get a few pieces of candy for them to eat on the way to the park. Some of the parents wondered why Lacie didn't have any kids counting that she loved other people's kids so much.

She would just reply, "One day when God is ready for me to have them, then I will."

She did know that she wanted twin boys whenever she did have kids. Sometimes when there were no kids in the counselor's office, Lacie would sit in the nurse's office.

The school nurse was Sherrie Wiggins. She seemed like a nice lady

Miracle Bridges

and they had become close working with each other every day. Sherrie grew up as what they call an Army brat. Her dad was African American and her mom was Spanish. Sherrie's dad served in the military for 20 years while her mom was a stay-at-home mom. They had lived all over the world. They lived in Japan, New Mexico, Europe, North Carolina, Florida, and New York. They moved around a lot when she was growing up, but Tennessee was where she always wanted to be and now she had finally settled down.

Sherrie had only been working at the school for two years and she had no intentions on leaving anytime soon. She also worked part-time at a rehab center for females which was a few miles away from the school. Sherrie and Lacie would sit in the nurse's office and just tell life stories of how they grew up. Lacie liked Sherrie but still didn't get too personal with her. She knew she had to set boundaries between being co-workers and associates because she learned a long time ago that mixing work business with personal business could cause problems. Sherrie would sometimes try to hang out with Lacie outside of work. They would go out for coffee or something like that or maybe even go pick up a bite to eat on their lunch break, but other than that Lacie was very careful. Sherrie had a tendency of telling Lacie about some of the patients at the rehab and honestly, Lacie didn't want to hear it. Every time she heard something about rehab she would think about the last time she had seen Myra. She knew Myra was on drugs and tried to avoid talking about it with her, so it wouldn't make their relationship even worse than it was. However, she did remember that Myra was happy the last time she saw her. She was with Erin and she seemed like she was on cloud 9, but hey that was over years ago and she hadn't seen her since.

Lacie tried to contact Tyra several times, but it seemed like she was always busy working and it took forever for Tyra to return her calls.

After a while, Lacie stopped calling Tyra and just decided to let her live her life. Lacie even tried looking for Erin. She thought that maybe Erin would have known where Myra was. She had only met him once, but never forgot his name or his face. She got on Facebook one day and searched for his name and was surprised when it came up. She figured since Myra was so happy with him the last time she saw them together that he had to know where she was. So, she inboxed him several times within a week but didn't get a response. This had her worried because Mable hadn't heard from Myra either and it was truly impossible for a person to just disappear. So, where was she?

A week later, she got back on Facebook and to her surprise, Erin had replied to her message. As she read his message, she realized that he didn't know where she was either. Erin had been back in Tennessee for almost three years and hadn't seen Myra anywhere, but they decided to exchange numbers and to keep each other posted if either one of them heard anything from Myra. After work, Lacie called her uncle Johnathan to see if he heard anything or to see if Tyra maybe had mentioned Myra to him, but he didn't hear anything either.

It was now the beginning of January. Lacie's office was always busy from the months of October to March. It seemed as if, kids had so much on their minds after the holidays. Of course, some children would come to her office just to speak to her and to get out of class. Even in Sherrie's office, it was a little boy who would come in at least twice a week. Sometimes, nothing would even be wrong with him. He would ask to eat lunch in her office, so he could watch the mini size TV that was in the corner by her desk. Sometimes, she would have cartoons playing to help some of the kids feel better when they were indeed sick.

One day, Lacie was on her way to her office but was stopped in her tracks. She saw a little boy crying and wanted to know what was wrong. She tried to comfort him in an appropriate way, but on the inside, she just wanted to hold him and tell him that whatever was wrong that it would be okay.

He looked up at her and said, "Some of the kids keep teasing me, saying that my mommy doesn't want to bring me to school because she's embarrassed of me."

"Oh, Sweetie that's not true, I'm sure that your mommy loves you."

With tears dripping down his cheeks he managed to say, "If she loves me, then why doesn't she want to see me? I have never seen my mommy face to face. I have only seen pictures of her. I see a lot of kids with both of their parents and it makes me sad. My daddy says that God will bring her back to us, but it's hard to believe that. Do you believe that?" Lacie looked at him speechless because she had never met his mom or dad.

Lacie took his little hands into hers and said, "Sweetie, anything is possible with God if you believe. God can bring your mommy back to you and your dad."

As she got up to grab him some Kleenex, he asked her if could she pray with him. Although it was against school policy, she couldn't send him back to his class without praying for him. So, she sat down next to him and softly prayed. After they finished praying, he walked out of her office and headed to class.

CHAPTER 9

Nothing Happens by Accident

One day during recess, Erin Jr. was full of energy and was having tons of fun. He was playing with the basketball until he fell and scraped his left knee. The gym teacher sent him directly to the nurse's office to get checked and bandaged.

When he arrived at the nurse's office, Sherrie was just getting back from her lunch break. When he walked in, she just smiled and asked him what was wrong. He pulled up his left pants leg and showed her the little scrap he had just gotten. It wasn't that bad at all, but she still needed to clean it and bandage it to keep it from getting infected. When she was done cleaning the scrap, he gave her a big hug and walked out the door to go back to his class. When Sherrie got up to close the door behind him, she noticed that he had dropped a picture. On the picture, it was a woman and a man. They appeared to be acting silly in the picture as if they were having a lot of fun. Sherrie continued to stare at the picture. The lady in the picture looked very familiar to Sherrie for some reason, and she couldn't think where she had seen her. Suddenly, she was startled out of her thoughts by some students that were walking down the hall laughing loudly. She decided to turn on the TV and drink a bottle of water.

Later that day, when school was dismissed, she stood outside the exit doors where the students usually came through to wait for their rides. She waited for about 10 minutes before she saw Erin Jr.'s class being dismissed. She wanted to pull him over to the side to give him his picture back.

"Hey, Erin! I just wanted to give you your picture back. You dropped it earlier when you were in my office."

"Thanks a lot, Ms. Wiggins."

"If you don't mind me asking Sweetie, who is that in that picture?"

"It's my mommy and daddy. My daddy gave it to me, so I would never forget my mommy."

"And where is your mommy Erin?"

Erin looked at the ground because he didn't know the answer to her question. He looked back up and noticed that his dad was just pulling up to pick him up. He looked at Sherrie and then ran to the car. Sherrie couldn't understand why she was suddenly overtaken by sadness. She wondered what was the cause of the devastating look that she saw on his face when she asked him about his mother. Was she dead? Was she in jail or did she walk out of his life? She couldn't figure it out, but all she knew was that she couldn't get the picture out of her head.

Since it was Thursday, she knew it was Lacie's turn to pay for coffee, so she headed to her office. When she arrived at Lacie's office she saw that Lacie had her back turned. So, she decided to sneak up on her and scare her a bit but made a mistake when she stumbled over Lacie's briefcase.

Lacie turned around and bursts out laughing saying, "See, you tried to scare me and almost fell. God don't like the ugly Sherrie." Sherrie caught her balance and managed to give Lacie a playful shove.

"So, are you ready to go grab some coffee? You do know it's your turn to pay." Lacie looked at Sherrie knowing that she wouldn't forget that.

"Yeah, I meant to call you at your office earlier. I was thinking that we could just go by my house and have coffee," Sherrie was shocked because Lacie had never invited her to her house for as long as they known each other, "my mom gave me a recipe for this homemade pound cake and I made it yesterday evening."

Sherrie started licking her lips and rubbing her stomach and said, "I'm down with that. Cake and coffee, sound great!" I guess Lacie was finally getting comfortable with Sherrie because she had never invited her over before.

"Well, give me a few minutes and then we can leave. You can follow behind me."

When they arrived at Lacie's apartment, she checked the mail and went inside. Lacie had recently moved into her own two bedroom apartment. She had wanted her own space and plus, it was only 5 minutes away from Mable's house. While Lacie set up the coffee maker, Sherrie decided to look around a bit. She admired the paintings that Lacie had in the living room. Lacie had fine taste in art plus, the price was very cheap, so she bought it. Sherrie was impressed with Lacie's decor, but one picture stood out the most. It was a picture of her and two other girls. Sherrie examined the picture for about three minutes and then turned around to ask Lacie who the girls were in the picture.

A slight smile seemed to appear on Lacie's face when she replied, "Those are my sisters. We took that picture when we were much younger."

Sherrie trying to be sarcastic replied, "Of course, it was when you all were much younger. You had pigtails plus, you had better taste in clothing back then." Lacie laughed as well.

She knew that her appearance had changed quite a bit. Well, maybe more than a bit. Lacie's definition of dressing comfortably was simply a pair of sweatpants and a t-shirt. For work, she would throw on a simple blouse and black pants. Lacie didn't date much. Her main focus was on

Miracle Bridges

the kids at school along with taking care of Mable. Sherrie asked Lacie simple questions about her sisters, like what were they're names and where did they live now. She told Sherrie that Tyra lived in California and Myra used to stay in Tennessee and that she had been trying to contact her. Before they could say anything else the coffee was ready which almost took Sherrie's attention off the picture. Sherrie loved the smell of fresh coffee. She would mix a little caramel creamer in hers that reminded her of being in a bakery. Sherrie started to sip her coffee but picked the picture back up. She has had two pictures encounters within a 24-hour period. Also, in both pictures, it almost looked like the same girl, but it couldn't be or could it?

Sherrie and Lacie enjoyed two cups of coffee and ate a slice of a cake. Sherrie loved the way Lacie baked the cake. It was really moist. She tried to get the recipe out of her, but Lacie wouldn't let her have it since it was a family recipe. They sat and joked a bit before it was time for Sherrie to go to work at the rehab center. She did therapy sessions there on Mondays and Thursdays. They gave each other a hug and Lacie walked Sherrie to the door.

"Thanks for coming over, I really enjoyed it, Girl. If you're not doing anything tomorrow, maybe we can do it again."

"That would be awesome, tomorrow is my lazy day, so same time tomorrow?" They both agreed and departed ways.

Lacie decided to go check on Mable. When she arrived, Mable was in her bed lying down. She had been sleeping a lot lately and barely ever wanted to eat anything, but she was happy to see Lacie. She always looked forward to seeing Lacie. Lacie would sometimes massage her feet and prepare dinner for her. Mable's health was really confusing. Sometimes, she would feel okay and other times she would feel horrible. Mable had finally confided in Lacie and told her that she had cancer. Lacie was sad, but she knew that her mother needed her more now than ever. Not only to do things around the house but to also be there for mental support. Sometimes, Lacie would spend the night and lay in the bed with Mable until they both fell asleep. They would watch movies and reflect on the older days when they were little girls. Lacie had given Mable her dinner for the night and made sure she had her meds before she left. Seeing that Mable was all set, she kissed her on the cheek and said her goodbyes. Lacie locked the door behind her and headed back home.

 Meanwhile, Sherrie had arrived at work and was ready to start her meeting. The meeting was held every 2 weeks, so there were different people in every meeting. Some rehab residents would complete their six months, some would leave because detoxing became too hard for them. Therefore, they would end up back on drugs and overdosing from it. Some would even leave and then come back within days claiming that they wanted help. However, no matter what the reason was, Sherrie was always dedicated to helping them. You wouldn't believe that some of the rehab residents used to be doctors, teachers, cooks, or abuse victims in general. Some of them had gotten to the point where you couldn't even recognize them.

 When it was time for the meeting to begin everyone found a seat in the circle of chairs in the center of the room. It was about 12 people in the group this time which was twice as small as to what the groups usually consists of. Everyone had to say their names, where they were from, and what drug they wanted to be delivered from. As they went around the circle, Sherrie's attention was caught on this one lady. She had only been there for a few weeks. As the lady spoke quietly, Sherrie continued to stare at her. When the meeting was over. Sherrie asked the lady to stay a little longer, so they could talk.

After everyone had left, Sherrie sat down next to her and began a conversation.

"Hey, Sweetie my name is Sherrie. What did you say your name was?"

"My name is Myra."

Sherrie was shocked by the woman words. Was this a coincidence or was this the lady that was in the pictures that she had seen earlier that day. Before saying another word, Myra stood up motioning that she had somewhere to go. Myra smiled at Sherrie and walked out the door. Sherrie sat there for a while trying to collect her thoughts. She didn't know what was really happening, but she was going to find out.

The next day, when she arrived at work she was anxious to ask little Erin more about the lady in the picture. She had gotten permission to pull him out of class for a brief moment. She brought him into her office and closed the door behind them.

"Hey, Erin how is your day going so far?"

"It's going great," replied Erin, "I had my favorite breakfast this morning. My daddy made me pancakes with bananas and it was good!" Sherrie laughed at the excitement he had in his voice.

"Erin, do you remember the picture you dropped in my office the other day? You said that the two people in the picture were your mommy and daddy, right?"

"Yes, Mam."

"What are their names?"

Little Erin looked at her and said, "Me and my daddy have the same name. He is big Erin and I am little Erin. My mommy name is Myra. She couldn't be a lady Erin because that's a boy name."

Sherrie laughed at Erin because he really had a sense of humor to be a little child, but more so she was shocked that this lady who she met last night at the rehab center looked just like the woman in Erin's picture and had the same name. She wasn't a rocket scientist, but she knew that the Myra at the rehab center was indeed the same Myra in Erin's picture which meant that she was his mother.

Sherrie jumped ahead of herself and said, "I think I know who your mother is and most important I know where she is."

Erin's eyes lit up like fireworks he was very excited. His father had been looking for his mom for a while and now some one finally knew where she was.

It was almost time for Erin's class to go to the library. So, Sherrie gave Erin a hall pass to go back to his classroom. Sherrie had felt some sort of relief. She decided to type up a letter and addressed it to little Erin's dad to let him know the news. She was completely over joyed.

When school let out Sherrie gave little Erin the letter to put in his bookbag and reminded him to give it to his dad. She went back to her office to shut everything down, so she could meet Lacie at her office and they could leave. Sherrie was looking forward to more of Lacie's homemade pound cake. When she arrived at Lacie's office Lacie was preparing to leave as well. Lacie double checked to make sure that everything was turned off before they left the office.

As they pulled up in her driveway, Mable called her on her cell phone. She needed Lacie to pick up a prescription for her. So, Sherrie parked her car at Lacie's house and rode with her to the drug store. Sherrie didn't know much about Mable, but she was ready to meet her. Lacie went through the drive-through to pick up Mable's meds and went straight to Mable's house. When they got inside Mable was sitting on the couch talking on the phone with Tyra. Lacie didn't want to disturb her, so she put the meds beside Mable and gave her a kiss on the cheek. Sherrie didn't get a chance to talk to Mable, but she could tell that she was sick in some way.

When they got to Lacie's house, Sherrie noticed a scrap book that Lacie must have been working on. So, she decided to scan through it and to her surprise, the mystery lady showed up again. Lacie noticed that she had an urgent voicemail on her house phone, so she checked it. Sherri continued to look at the pictures. Lacie pushed play thinking that it was just another bill collector but was thrown off track to hear that it was Erin. She hadn't talked to him in about 8 months and when they did talk it was only for about 2 minutes to see if she heard anything from Myra.

"Hey Lacie this is Erin, I was calling you to let you know that I may have some information about Myra, call me back when you get a chance."

Sherrie froze when the voice message came to an end. Lacie turned around and saw the crazy look on her face.

Sherrie just kept saying, "This can't be real! This can't be happening!"

"Sherrie what's wrong. What can't be real, what can't be happening?"

Sherrie turned around and looked at Lacie and said, "You may want to sit down for this."

They had a seat while it was complete silence at first. Lacie didn't know what to expect.

"The other day in my office there was a little boy named Erin. He came to my office because he had a scrape on his knee. After I cleaned it and sent him back to his class, I noticed that he had dropped a picture on the floor. It was a picture of a man and a woman that appeared to be a couple. I kept looking at the photo because the lady looked very familiar. So, after school was dismissed, I pulled little Erin to the side to ask him who was this in the picture. He said it was his mother and father, and that his dad gave him the picture so that he wouldn't forget his mother."

"Ok, so what's so shocking about that Sherrie?"

"Wait there's more. The other day when I came to your house and I was looking at the pictures. You told me that the two girls in the picture with you were your twin sisters Myra and Tyra. I thought she looked familiar, but I brushed it off. Well, after I left your house, I had to hold a meeting at the rehab center. In the meeting, one of the women's name was Myra and she looked like the lady in the picture little Erin had. So, when I got to the school today, I pulled Erin out of class to ask him about his parents. He told me that his father name is Erin and his mother name is Myra and I knew then that it wasn't just a coincidence. I knew that was little Erin's mother. I sent home a letter for his dad stating that I have information about his mother and how to get in contact with her."

"So that's great Sherrie, you found his mother."

"Don't you see what's going on Lacie? I think this is your sister who you have been trying to contact. The same Myra in your scrapbook is the same Myra in little Erin's picture, and is the same Myra that is a patient at the rehab center that I work at."

Lacie looked confused, but manage to say, "It can't be the same Myra, Sherrie. My sister don't have any kids."

"How do you know Lacie? You said you haven't heard from her in how many years? Anything could have happened since then. I think you should call that guy Erin to see where this leads to. I included my number in the letter, so I'm sure he's going to call me."

Lacie picked up the phone and called Erin, but it went to his voicemail. Within seconds, Sherrie's phone rang and it was Erin. He sounded very happy on the other end and was anxious to get more information about Myra. Sherrie told him that a lady named Myra who was a patient at the rehab center may have been the same lady that he has been looking for. They talked a little bit and hung up.

Not even two minutes later, Lacie's phone rang and to her surprise it was Erin. He instantly started telling her all the information that he had gotten from Sherrie. Lacie was so shocked at all of what was going on, but at the same time she felt happy that she had finally knew something about where Myra was. Now, the next thing for Lacie to do was get in touch with Myra, but because it would put Sherrie's job at risk she knew she couldn't meet with her there. She tried calling California several times to talk to Tyra to see if she had information about Myra. I guess Tyra got tired of Lacie calling her and finally called her back, but she didn't know anything either. Tyra knew that Myra was trying to keep things on a low profile but didn't understand why. Lacie recommended that Tyra fly out as soon as she could. Everything was a bit too much to handle for her. Mable was sick with cancer and now finding out that her sister had a secret child. She knew that things needed to come to the light because not only were relationships being affected, but a child's life was being affected. Lacie suggested that Sherrie go with her to her mother's house the next day to explain everything that was going on and she agreed to do so. Lacie called Erin and asked him to meet her there as well, but was anyone ready for what was about to unfold?

CHAPTER 10

What's Done in the Dark Comes to the Light

The next day, they picked up Tyra from the airport and headed straight to Mable's house. When they arrived at Mable's house she was in the living room watching TV and drinking a glass of sweet tea with lemon. It was something she did at least twice a week for relaxation. When she noticed, Tyra walking in behind Lacie and Sherrie she thought she was seeing things. She quickly got up and hugged Tyra tightly and kissed her continuously on each cheek. She started to calm down a bit when she saw the look on Lacie's face. She knew her daughter well and knew that something was wrong.

"What's wrong Lacie? What is bothering you, Sweetie?" Lacie walked over and gently squeezed Mable's hand and looked into her eyes.

"Mama there is something that you should know."

"Okay Sweetheart, tell me what's wrong?"

"It's about Myra."

"Oh no, Lacie please don't tell me she's hurt? What happened to her?"

"Mama Myra is fine. I'm not sure if you remember a few years back when Myra came by with a guy named Erin."

"Yeah, I remember that he was such a sweet guy and Myra seemed to be happy, but why is he important?"

"Well, first off Mama, I want you to officially meet Sherrie. Sherrie and I work at the school together, but Sherrie also works at a rehab center for women. Erin and I have been keeping in contact with each other, in case we heard anything from Myra. We couldn't find out anything until Sherrie found out that Myra was a patient at the same rehab she works at." Tyra interrupted her.

"What do you mean a patient at a rehab? Myra don't do drugs, Lacie. Myra told me that she has been living with a friend and has been just focusing on making life better that's why she been so busy."

As the words left Tyra's mouth she just lowered her head realizing what Lacie was saying had to be true. Everything started to make sense to Tyra. Lacie looked at Tyra and continued with the story.

"Well, there's a little boy that goes to our school named Erin Jr. Sherri noticed one day that he dropped a picture and the lady in the picture looked very familiar. She found Erin Jr. after school to give him the picture back and to ask him who was in the picture. Erin told Sherrie that it was his mother and father and that their names were Erin and Myra.

Mable froze as she uttered, "Are you trying to tell me that Myra had a son and kept him a secret all this time?"

"Yes, Mama that's exactly what I'm saying."

Tyra started to tear up and asked, "Well, where is he?" As soon as she words left her lips they were startled by a knock on the door.

Lacie looked at Tyra and replied, "That should be them now." Lacie got up and opened the door for Erin.

He had left little Erin in the car until he knew for sure that everything was okay. When he walked in and saw Tyra he thought it was Myra until Lacie told him that it was Myra's twin. Erin was completely shocked. He didn't know that Myra had a twin. He never asked and she never told him. They talked for a few minutes to get a better understanding of what was going on. Although Mable was disappointed that Myra would keep something like that from them, she was still excited to meet her grandson. Erin went to the car and brought him inside the house.

When little Erin walked into the house and saw Tyra, he ran straight to her hugging her tightly yelling, "Mommy! Mommy! I knew you would never forget me!"

Tyra looked at Lacie and just held him and cried. The excitement on his face and the joy he appeared to have was overwhelming. Tyra couldn't bring herself to tell him that she wasn't his mommy, but instead she was his auntie.

She turned him around and said, "This is your grandmother." Mable looked at him and grabbed his little hands.

"It's good to meet you Erin Jr."

Little Erin just smiled as he looked at his daddy and said, "See Daddy God always answer prayers no matter how long it takes." Erin smiled and agreed.

Tyra got up and walked to the back to call Myra. She knew if she told Myra what was taking place at Mable's house then she would never come. So, she didn't tell her. She just told her that she was in town and wanted to set up a dinner date for them. That day, everyone had found some sense of peace except Myra.

Little Erin spent the night with Tyra at Mable's house. Tyra and little Erin stayed up talking, they watched cartoons and played board games. He had a blast! He thought that his mommy had finally came back to him. When he asked questions about Myra it broke Tyra's heart into pieces because she couldn't answer them. How could Myra, her own twin hide something like this from her? She just couldn't understand it.

The next day, Erin came to pick up Erin Jr. and took him to school. Lacie went with Mable to her doctor's appointment at the Cancer Treatment Center. When they arrived at the doctor's office Lacie noticed that Mable appeared to be weaker than usual. She held her by her arm and

Miracle Bridges

assisted with helping her into the doctor's office. However, Mable insisted she was fine and ensured Lacie that it was because she didn't eat breakfast. The doctor had called them to the back within 10 minutes. Mable was always on time for her appointments. The doctor did his usual routine with Mable and wrote her another prescription to lower her blood pressure. Lacie pulled the doctor to the side as he came out of the room and asked him about Mable's health. He didn't want to be blunt, but he knew that Lacie was the oldest and the closest to Mable and she needed to know what was going on. He knew that Mable had less than three months to live. When he told Lacie, she just stood there as if she had seen a ghost. Lacie felt a pain inside her chest like she never felt before. Mable knew she was dying and didn't want to worry the girls. She just wanted to let things happen peacefully.

Lacie went back in the room and made sure that Mable had everything she needed. When they got in the car, Lacie decided to ask her about her health to see what she was going to say. Lacie knew her mother was sick but didn't know how serious it was. Mable tried to beat around the bush but noticed that Lacie knew her state of condition when she saw the tears dripping down her face.

"So, I'm guessing you already spoke with Dr. Miles."

"Yes, I did Mama. Were you going to tell us that you are dying Mama?"

"Honestly, no Lacie. I didn't want to tell you girls that. I just wanted to go peacefully. It's bad enough that you girls are all split up. I never thought things would get this bad between my girls. You girls grew up so close. Lacie, I prayed and prayed and prayed that you and your sister's relationship would be reconciled. Telling you and the others would have only made things worse."

"Mama that's not true. I think it would have brought us closer if anything. You know we love you Mama and will put our differences aside and come together to be there for you."

"That's the thing, Lacie I don't want the differences put aside, I want them to cease period or to be resolved. Life is too short to live in anger and hate. I want you girls to come together by all means and let go of the nonsense."

At this point, they were pulling up in the drive way. Lacie helped Mable into the house and made her some lunch. Lacie made sure that Mable had everything she needed and then headed out the door to meet Sherrie at the school.

While Mable was enjoying her lunch, the twins were on the other side of town enjoying theirs. Myra was so happy to see Tyra when she walked into the restaurant. They greeted each other with kisses and proceeded to sit down. They talked and laughed hysterically. Meanwhile, Tyra tried to beat around the bush to get information from Myra about what she had been up to and if there was anything she needed to tell her. I guess she wanted her to be up front and to see if Myra would really tell her everything like they used to do when they were younger. Myra played it cool as if everything was going great with her. Tyra couldn't understand how Myra could sit right there in her face and tell a bold face lie. Everything was not great, in fact, everything was coming to the light and Myra just couldn't see or even imagine how crazy things were about to get. Tyra looked at her watch and motioned like she had somewhere to be in a hurry. She suggested that Myra come by the house later to see Mable. Myra knew she hadn't seen Mable in a while and felt a little bad about it.

So, she agreed to go. They planned to meet there around 4 pm which was just a few hours away. They gave each other a hug and Myra went her way while Tyra went hers.

When Tyra got back to the house Mable was lying down. She had been weak all day and needed to get a little rest before Erin Jr. came over after school. Little Erin was a very energetic little boy, so she knew she needed to reserve her strength. Although she had just met her grandson, she had already fallen in love with him already. She thought that he had Myra's eyes and that made her think of James because Myra had James' eyes.

Tyra laid on the bed beside Mable and rubbed her head gently asking her if she was okay. Tyra had been in California for years, so she noticed a big change in her mother. Once again, Mable insisted that she was okay, so they both laid there and took a nap.

CHAPTER 11

Things Get Worse Before They Get Better

Several hours later, they were awakened by a knock on the door and little Erin's voice laughing at a 'knock knock' joke his dad had told him. Tyra got up, stretched, and then proceeded to open the door.

Little Erin ran in and hugged her saying, "Mommy how was your day?"

Tyra just smiled and said, "Fine Sweetie."

Erin looked at her with a slight smile and nodded his head in a way that told Tyra thank you. He knew that it must hurt Tyra to have to pretend that she was Myra in order to spare Erin Jr.'s feelings, but Tyra knew this couldn't go on for much longer. Here goes her nephew thinking that she was his mommy. Myra needed to step up to the plate fast and take responsibility as a mother or at least tell him the truth. This little boy was in love with her and she had no idea because she wasn't around. They all sat down and waited for Mable to come into the living room.

When she got into the living room and sat down little Erin ran to her and gave her a big kiss on the cheek saying, "Guess what Grandma? I made the little league baseball team." He was so excited and Mable was excited for him.

They sat there while Erin Jr. went on and on about the baseball team and what happened at school that day.

About 15 minutes later, Lacie walked through the door. She had just gotten back from her meeting with Sherrie. Lacie sat down and joined them while she chatted about little Erin and him joining the baseball team. Since it was a pretty day, Mable offered everyone lemonade and pound cake. Everyone got up and headed to the back yard to sit on the patio and enjoy the weather. She started to cut a slice of cake but stopped because it was another knock at the door. Before she had a chance to get to it and open it, it slowly came open. Mable couldn't believe her eyes. It was Myra!

Myra smiled and managed to utter, "Hey Mama, how are you doing?"

Mable held out her arms to embrace her daughter as tears dripped down her cheeks. Myra asked where Tyra was and she told her that they were on the back porch.

"They who? Who are they?"

Before she could answer, Myra walked passed her and headed to the back yard. As soon as she reached the door that led to the patio Lacie walked in.

"Wow, hey Myra. What are you doing here?"

"Didn't know I had to have permission to come over Mama's house, Lacie."

"I didn't mean it in a negative way Myra, I am just surprised that you are here, that's all."

Lacie looked at Mable with concern, but Mable just smiled. Everything was about to come to the light.

"Tyra asked me to come by, so I'm here."

"Okay, just wait right here Myra, let me get her for you." Myra looked at Lacie disgusted.

"Stop it, Myra!" Mable knew exactly what was going through Myra's head.

"Stop what Mama? I haven't seen Lacie in how long now and this is the type of welcome I get."

"Well, I didn't see or hear you say anything to her as well." Lacie and Tyra walked in the house.

"Hey Sis, you made it," replied Tyra, "come on in the back."

Lacie looked at Tyra and asked, "Are you sure that's a good idea, Tyra?"

"Yeah, why not? She has to know what's going on sooner or later and we have to settle this immediately."

"Settle what?" Myra asked confusingly.

Before they could answer, Erin walked into the house to get a cup of ice for his lemonade. Myra looked into Erin's face and froze for at least 30 seconds without saying anything.

"What are you doing here Erin? Is this some type of set up or something? Tyra was you in on this?" Mable tried to reach out to her for a hug, but she snatched away.

"You told me to come here for what reason Tyra, huh?!" At this point, she was yelling.

Tyra opened the back door and looked outside while little Erin Jr. chased a butterfly.

Tyra looked back at Myra and said, "For that reason Myra. This little boy has a picture of you and Erin and whenever he sees me he hugs me and calls me mommy thinking I'm you. I can't take this anymore Myra. You have lied to me for years about a secret child, doing drugs, and even rehab." Myra looked into Tyra's eyes feeling a deep pain of betrayal.

"Erin, did you tell them tell them I was on drugs? Of course not Myra, I would never betray you."

"Then how did they know I was in rehab? It is supposed to be confidential?" So many things were running through Myra's mind.

Erin looked at her and said, "Calm down Myra, I know things seem crazy right now, but it wasn't supposed to happen this way."

"It shouldn't have happened at all Erin, you agreed to take the baby if I didn't get an abortion. You wanted me to have him! I told you that I wasn't ready to be a mother or even worst, don't know how to be a mother."

"I understand that Myra, but you completely disappeared. Lacie and I have been trying to find you. Just because we agreed that you would give me custody of Erin Jr. didn't mean that I didn't care about you or your well being Myra."

For some reason, Myra just completely lost it saying, "I don't know why Lacie was looking for me when she don't care about me, she never cared about me." Lacie stopped Myra from speaking any further.

"What do you mean Myra? You are my sister. I know you're still holding on to what happened to you on your prom night, but I never meant for anything to happen to you. I love you and that will never change. I have longed for our relationship to be healed the night that it happened, but you never forgave me."

Before any one could say anything else all eyes turned to Mable as she collapsed on the floor. Myra grabbed the house phone and called the ambulance while Lacie and Tyra checked her pulse. They put a cold rag on her head until the ambulance arrived. Within 25 minutes they arrived at the hospital. Mable was now conscious but was still very weak. They had her hooked up to several machines. That night was very overwhelming for everyone.

Tyra went back to Mable's house to get some rest. They had planned to take shifts with staying with Mable while she was in the hospital. Lacie and Myra stayed at the hospital with Mable that night. While Mable was sleeping, Lacie decided to break the silence between her and Myra.

"Myra, we need to talk. If you still decide not to talk to me after this then that's your choice, but at least hear me out. I understand that you are still upset about what happened to you, but I want you to understand that I would never put you in harm's way. Since the day that happened, I have been praying for reconciliation between us. I love you, Myra. We will always be sisters and I'm sure if we just put things in God's hand that He can fix them." Myra looked at Lacie with tears in her eyes.

"How can God fix this Lacie? I am in rehab and I had a child out of wedlock that don't even know who I am. I am just a mess, period. I'm sure that I am too big of a mess for God to fix."

Mable who they thought were asleep startled them when she started to speak, "Myra, God don't need us to try to fix things before we give our mess to Him Sweetie. He wants us to come to Him as we are. As much as you loved your father Myra, he wasn't always the man he was when he died. Me and your grandmother Mae used to pray for your father all the time. With God's help, he was able to give his mess to Jesus and become a new creation, and the same thing can happen to you. I remember how close you girls were when you all were children. I miss that and I also have been praying since that incident happened to you that God would fix things. I know things may seem a little crazy right now, but things work for the good of those who love the Lord. I just want all the fighting to stop. It's true that blood is thicker than water and family needs to stick together, but the Blood of Jesus is thicker and can mend any brokenness in any family. Think about it Myra, you are broken and you want God to forgive you right?" Myra shook her head yes.

"Well then, forgive your sister. It's time for you girls to move forward. Myra, it's time for you be the mother that you're supposed to be. That boy loves you and wants a relationship with you."

Before Mable could say anything else Myra stood up and went over to hug Lacie. She hugged her so tight that she could barely breathe. They were at a hospital and healing takes place in hospitals, even though they never knew how sick they really were.

After talking for a few more minutes, Mable suggested that they head home to get some rest and come back tomorrow. She kissed them on the cheek and told each one of them that she loved them. They turned the light off and headed out the door. Lacie suggested that Myra stay at Mable's house instead of going back to the rehab.

When they arrived there, Tyra was sleeping like a baby. They both laid in Mable's bed and went to sleep. When morning came, they were awakened by the neighbor's dog barking. Lacie looked at the clock and saw that it was 7:45 am and visitation at the hospital started at 9. They all got up and had morning devotion together like they used to do before heading back to the hospital to see Mable. When they got there they found out they Mable had passed away that morning at 7:52 am. So, while the girls were having devotion and worship, Mable was taking her last few breaths. The doctor had tried to call Lacie's phone to give her the news, but her phone had died last night and she never got a chance to put it on the charger. The girls were completely devastated. Lacie knew Mable was dying but didn't expect it to be so soon.

As Tyra started to cry Myra looked at her and said, "Do you all remember when daddy died mommy told us that nothing happens without God's say so? Well, I guess God said it was time for Mama to leave us girls. I know it hurts, but just knowing that mama's prayers were answered last night gives me peace."

"Your right Myra, besides mama didn't want to worry you all, but she knew that she only had a few months to live anyway. So, I am just glad that she's not in pain anymore. It's going to be hard of course, but we have each other, and we have God, and with Him, we can make it through anything. The girls hugged each other and left the hospital to break the news to everyone else. They started making the funeral arrangements.

When they arrived back at Mable's house, they sat around and talked about old memories. Erin had come by to check on the girls but left Erin Jr. in the car. Tyra welcomed him in and asked where her favorite little guy was. Erin replied that he was in the car and he wanted to see if it was okay with Myra for him to come in first. Myra looked at her sisters and nodded her head for Erin to go get him from the car. For the first time, little Erin would meet his real mother and not just his auntie.

When he walked into the house and saw another lady that looked just like his mommy he was very confused. He asked if he had two mommies and every one laughed hysterically. Tyra looked at Myra giving her the encouragement to take over the conversation.

Myra looked in little Erin's eyes and said, "No Sweetie, you only have one mommy. I am your mommy."

At this point, her emotions were running wild which caused Myra to tear up. Erin Jr. walked over to the couch Myra was sitting at and wiped her cheek.

"It's okay Mommy, you don't have to cry. I don't need two mommies." Myra smirked, loving Erin Jr.'s innocence.

Myra grabbed his face softly and asked him if he would forgive her for not being there for him and if he would give her another chance to be a good mommy.

Erin Jr. looked at her and said, "I forgive you, Mommy. I knew you would come back to me and Daddy. I had a dream that you came back and we were happy and eating ice cream."

Myra thought back to the dream she had about her father and how it came true. She knew that God had a special way of speaking to certain people. Myra looked up at big Erin and he gave her a smile that said all was forgiven.

They spent the rest of the day making phone calls and making funeral arrangements. Erin made a phone call to his Pastor to see if they could have the funeral at his church and he agreed. He asked if it was okay that he came over to pray with the family since he was around the area and they accepted his offer.

When he got there, Erin welcomed him in and introduced him to everyone. Well, re-introduced them that is. His Pastor just so happened to be Pastor Edward Jones, the same guy that took Tyra to the prom. The same one that she broke up with because she moved to California and wanted to focus on college. When he spoke to her she was completely speechless at how much he had changed. She would have never thought that he would become a pastor. He prayed for everyone as he had come to do, but before he left the house he pulled Tyra to the side to talk to her. He wanted to see how things were going and how she was holding up. He also wanted to invite her out to dinner. Although Tyra was totally against dating anyone, she felt like she knew him half of her life and accepted the invitation.

After he left, Sherrie came by to check on everyone as well. Little did she know that Myra would be there at the same time. When she walked into the house Myra just stood there in shock. Myra knew then how everyone had found out that she was in rehab.

She walked over and extended her hand, "The name is Sherrie, right? You work at the rehab center."

"Yes, I do. But what are you doing here?"

Sherrie didn't know how to answer, so Lacie spoke up for her, "Sherrie and I work together at the school. Plus, she's a really good friend of mines, and honestly Myra, she's the one that came across the picture that little Erin dropped at school that had you and Erin in it. She noticed you were the same one in the photo albums that I have at my apartment."

"Is that why you asked who I was at the end of the meeting? You knew exactly what was going on didn't you?"

"Yeah, I did, but please don't report me, I love my job at the rehab center."

"Report you! I'm not going to report you, I think all of this was in God's divine plan. You helped bring my family back together, so how could I ever be mad at you for that." Sherrie looked at Lacie and smiled.

Sherrie stayed at the house for a few hours helping the girls with whatever they needed. Meanwhile, Myra walked outside to get some fresh air but was startled by Erin who was coming from behind the house.

"Sorry Sweetie, I didn't mean to scare you."

"Its okay," Myra replied, "what were you doing back there anyway?"

"I was in the garage getting out the lawn mower. Your mom asked me if I could cut the grass a few days ago and I told her I would." Myra smiled and said thanks for keeping your word.

He gently grabbed Myra's arm and said, "I always keep my word, especially when I told you that I would always love you." Myra smiled.

"How could you love me after leaving you to raise your child on your own."

"That's because I never thought of him as my child. I thought of him as our child Myra. Although we had him out of wedlock he is still our child. I asked God to forgive me and to bring you back to us, so I could do things the right way. I didn't know how He was going to do it, but by the look of things He already did it."

"You know what Erin, you're right. He did bring us back together and I know you still love me. I have decided to give my life to God which means that the only way we could be together is if we got married."

Erin smiled and replied, "We can make that happen, Myra. A few days ago, when I stopped by your mom's house to pick up Erin Jr. she asked me did I love still love you and I told her yes. I told her that I wanted to marry you one day and she told me that I had her blessing. Also, she believed that God would bring you back to me and little Erin. For a lady not to know me very long she sure was kind-hearted and nice. I told her that if I ever got a chance to see you again that I would never let you go and that I would make you my wife."

"Erin, do you really understand what you're saying? Marriage is a life time commitment."

"I know exactly what I'm saying Myra. Will you give me another chance and let me be the man I always wanted to be to you?"

Myra looked into his eyes and said, "Yes!"

She couldn't believe what she had just done, but she was stepping out on faith. In the same day, she lost her mother and accepted an engagement. She knew that if God was with them then who could be against them.

Myra ran into the house to tell everyone the good news. To some people arranging a funeral would have been a sad thing, but not to them. It was more of a celebration. They knew Mable had been baptized and did everything she could to lead her kids to Christ and that she would be called up when Jesus came back. Everything that Mable had prayed for before she died had come true. So, her death wasn't a sad thing at all.

Over the next couple of years, things had changed drastically. Lacie accepted a position at Tennessee State teaching Psychology. Sherrie started an organization for battered women and drug abusers. Erin and Myra got married and moved in Mable's house after having a baby girl. Tyra and Pastor Jones were engaged. Johnathan and Janice even visited every 2 or 3 months. Everyone's relationship grew closer and closer. Every week they went to church together and had dinner afterwards. God had truly stepped in and worked things out for the good of those who love Him.

They had learned several lessons. If anyone believes and accepts Christ then they are a new creature. That God can fix anything that's broken. Pray, consistently until something happens. Your test is your testimony. God works in mysterious ways and much more.

Now they could be a blessing to someone else who may cross their paths with similar problems because God has equipped them and gave them life and life more abundantly. So, no matter how bad your past may seem just remember that Revelations: 12:11 says, "They overcame by the power of their testimonies" what we go through in life is not all about us but helping someone else realized that Jesus can clean up any mess and use them for His glory!

ABOUT THE AUTHOR

Miracle Bridges is a wife, a mother, a minister, but more importantly a child of God. She has a passion to save souls for the kingdom of God. Miracle has lived a life of brokenness, low self-esteem, betrayal, lust, and greed, but through the delivering power that God provides, she was able to come out of bondage and push forward to fulfill the purpose that God put in her. She believes from experience that things that never gets revealed, never get healed. That's why in this book "Their Problems but God's Promises" she speaks about things that most families are afraid to talk about. This book is filled with how you can be broken down and lost by greed, lust, drugs, unforgiveness, loss of a love one, wedlock, secrets and so much more. But most importantly, it shows the love of God and the power He has to make all things work together for the good of those that love Him. She has been in ministry with her husband Jason Bridges since 2010. Not only is she an author, but she is also a gospel rap artist, poet, and a motivational speaker that enjoys serving the homeless and blessing lives. Her prayer is that this book will bless you and lead you to follow Jesus.

www.ingramcontent.com/pod-product-compliance
Lightning Source LLC
Chambersburg PA
CBHW070631300426
44113CB00010B/1737